TWISTED SISTERS

How Four Superstorms Forever Changed the Northeast in 1954 & 1955

By

Eamon McCarthy Earls

Twisted Sisters: How Four Superstorms Forever Changed the Northeast in 1954 and 1955

ISBN 978-0-9825485-7-8

viaappiapress.com

Acknowledgements

This book was made possible through the efforts of many different people. At the University of Massachusetts-Amherst, I wish to thank Dr. Joel Wolfe of the History Department, and Maxine Schmidt, the University's excellent earth science librarian, for the resources and time that they contributed. Additionally, I wish to thank Dr. Marcus Waldron of the US Geological Survey--Northborough Water Science Center, the Boston Public Library Microform Department, the National Archives and Records Administration Boston Branch, and the Aspinock Historical Society of Putnam. I am tremendously grateful to Richard "Dick" Whitney, Southbridge historian and curator of the Optical Heritage Museum, and Bill Pearsall of the Aspinock Historical Society, whose images help to bring the 'Twisted Sisters' to life.

Contents

Introduction: History or Harbinger?

"'How could this happen?'...'Nothing like this ever happened before.'"

Stronger than the storm: it's a phrase that has caught on in the Mid-Atlantic states in the wake of the massive damage caused by Hurricane Sandy—dubbed a "superstorm" by the media-- in October, 2012. As New York and New Jersey rebuild their coastal communities after the multi-billion dollar storm, the phrase has nearly become the state motto.

Although the storm was highly destructive, few people in the Northeast realize that Sandy was far from unique. Sixty years ago, New England and the Northeast United States were slammed by four superstorms, back-to-back, that brought untold devastation to the region. These storms, coming at the tail end of a 16 year spate of superstorms, forever changed the way that the Northeast deals with hurricanes. They forever altered the fabric of many communities in Connecticut, Rhode Island, and Massachusetts, and changed the course of the region's history.

Besides the residents of New Orleans, Mobile and other Gulf Coast dwellers, few people in the modern US have experienced the kind of disruption created by Sandy in urban centers, small cities, and suburban towns. Whether or not Sandy's destructiveness was the result of global climate change, a 'perfect storm' of conditions, or a combination of many factors, the storm has served as a powerful reminder of the destructive strength of nature even in places far removed from the 'bath-tub' waters of the Caribbean. In modern

America, hurricanes are usually seen as a natural hazard limited to the southern US. In fact, many of the strongest and costliest hurricanes in US history have struck the sandy shoreline of the Northeastern US creating immense natural disasters.

New Englanders well versed in regional history and family stories may have grown up with tales of Hurricane of 1938 which arrived unexpectedly, destroying tens of thousands of homes, toppling whole forests, killing hundreds and inflicting damage in excess of four billion dollars. New Englanders also swap stories of a mid-winter calamity—the Blizzard of 1978. However, these accounts of destruction miss four key events in the 1950s.

By 1954, New Englanders were getting uncomfortably familiar with the unfriendly side of nature. In less than 20 years, the region had been battered by a series of particularly troublesome weather events, arriving at all times of year. In March, 1936, western New England and New Hampshire had experienced serious flooding, particularly in the Connecticut River Valley, as a result of extraordinary rains and tremendous snowmelt. Together, it became one of the costliest "freshets" on record.

Two years later, the Hurricane of 1938 left a path of destruction in its wake. In the midst of World War II, the Great Atlantic Hurricane of 1944 produced fully one-third of the damage caused by the terrible 1938 storm. Fortunately, with a greater awareness of hurricanes and legions of meteorologists tracking weather systems as a result of the war, casualties on land were limited. However, the storm still inflicted 100 million dollars of damage (1944 US dollars) and sent more than 300 mariners to watery graves along the

Eastern Seaboard. In 1950, Hurricane Dog passed close to Cape Cod knocking out power to homes. The year 1953 was marked by another storm. Hurricane Carol arrived in September, 1953, brushing the Maine coast with hurricane force winds before making landfall in Newfoundland. Fortunately, 1953's Carol was a comparatively "tame" storm that left little damage in its wake. It was a name that, when attached to a second storm, would soon gain more sinister connotations.

Then, things changed for the worse. As New England enjoyed the booming 1950s economy, four distinct hurricanes arriving between 1954 and 1955 brought about some of greatest damage ever seen from storms in America, at the time – or since.

Major tropical storms are only referred to as hurricanes within the region of the Atlantic Ocean. However, massive storms, with nearly identical characteristics form in the tropics across the globe—storms in the Northern Pacific that often affect China, the Philippines, Taiwan and Japan are described as typhoons, while storms in the Indian Ocean that impact Australia, India, and Bangladesh are termed cyclones.

Tropical cyclones in all their forms—hurricanes, typhoons and cyclones—form in "breeding grounds" that overlap the equator to the north and south. Atlantic cyclones frequently form in the Caribbean and around the Cape Verdean islands, off of West Africa.

In an average hurricane season, 10 tropical storms form from tropical depressions in the Gulf of Mexico, the Caribbean, and in some cases even the mid-Atlantic. Of the 10 storms that typically form, six will become hurricanes. Over a three year time span, five of these hurricanes will usually hit the US coastline, sometimes producing tremendous damage.

News meteorologists are usually keen to categorize new hurricanes based on their strength. Hurricanes are now categorized using the Saffir-Simpson Hurricane Scale, introduced in the 1970s. Meteorology is a vague science because of the complexities of weather systems. The scale attempts to combine measured wind speeds and damage into a metric that is easy to understand. For instance, a Category 1 hurricane is very similar to a tropical storm. With sustained winds between 74 and 95 miles per hour, a Category 1 hurricane is most likely to down branches and perhaps cause minor flooding in low-lying areas, if it is joined by heavy rainfall.

Unlike tornadoes, which can seem to appear as `bolts from the blue,' hurricanes are the end stage of massive weather systems. They develop from tropical depressions—areas where thick clouds of water vapor and thunderstorms mingle and begin to circulate. Within the depression, winds begin to pick up, reaching sustained speeds in the range of 40 miles per hour. Tropical storms are more intense than depressions. They feature well-organized clusters of thunderstorms that can circulate at speeds as high as 73 miles per hour. Tropical storms often make landfall causing damage consistent with weak hurricanes, bearing with them huge amounts of rain. A tropical storm is upgraded to hurricane status once it exceeds 74 miles per hour of sustained, circulating winds.

Each category correlates to higher winds and a higher chance of damage. Category 2 storms begin to cause property damage, tearing shingles and siding off of light-frame houses and flimsy mobile homes. Category 3 storms, including recent examples such as 2011's Hurricane Irene and 2012's Hurricane Sandy are far more dangerous, causing "extensive" damage, destroying mobile homes and generating more significant storm surges and flooding. Sandy proved that even mid-ranked storms can pack a tremendous punch.

The strongest and rarest hurricanes are Category 5 storms like the Hurricane of '38, or 1992's Hurricane Andrew in Florida. These massive storms are capable of destroying *all* wood frame buildings, leaving only masonry structures standing.

Where a hurricane strikes also matters. Many New England hurricanes have only grazed the region, raking Cape Cod, Martha's Vineyard and Nantucket with winds. Other storms have struck the land dead-on, with tracks that carry them across Rhode Island and southeastern Massachusetts to strike Boston, Providence and the large cities of the South Coast. The Narragansett Bay and Buzzards Bay are both particularly vulnerable areas as a result of their geography. Strong winds arriving from the south can easily funnel water up the bay as a storm surge, flooding cities and towns like Providence and Wareham.

Are the Twisted Sisters – the four closely sequenced storms of the 1950s -- simply a piece of novel regional history, or are they harbingers of much worse to come? Sixty years have passed since these storms arrived, with only the brief tumult of Donna, 1960, Belle, 1976, Gloria, 1985, Bob, 1991, and Irene, 2011, as hints of the kind of destruction that hurricanes can mete out. It has been a very long time since New Englanders witnessed a truly devastating hurricane, but a combination of history and cutting-edge climate science suggests that our region may be overdue.

Oceanographers and climatologists speak about a phenomenon known as Atlantic multidecadal oscillation (AMO). Researchers Schlesinger and Ramankutty recognized AMO in 1994, for the first time. Over time, the Atlantic's average sea surface temperature (SST) sea surface temperature oscillates by as much as a degree, for reasons unrelated to human greenhouse gas emissions and global climate change. The change seems to be due to slight alterations in thermohaline circulation—the network of warm and cold currents that circulate water within every ocean. In the Atlantic, this system includes the Gulf Stream, which delivers warm water to Europe (warm enough that palm trees are able to grow in Britain) and the North Atlantic Deep Water, which carries cold water south.

Because the oceans are a component of the climate and drivers of weather (along with sunlight) changes in SST are often tied to big changes in the weather. During times of SST increase, the US witnessed the awful Dust Bowl years of the 1930s on the Great Plains and the 10 year New England drought of the 1960s. But the trouble doesn't end there. Increased SST raises the likelihood that small hurricanes will develop into Category 4 or 5 superstorms, as slightly warmer surface waters evaporate more rapidly.

Almost all of the most serious hurricanes in the history of the Northeast have struck at times of positive AMO, when SST has risen above average. The hurricane seasons of 1954 and 1955 were notable peaks. The 1954 Atlantic hurricane season caused more damage than any season up to that time. Two named storms preceded Carol and Edna – one of them taking 55 lives around the Gulf of Mexico. A late September tropical storm dubbed Gilda killed 29 people after drenching northern Honduras. The worst hurricane of the season was Hurricane Hazel, which killed thousands in Haiti before striking the Carolinas in October, lumbering across much of the eastern US and striking Ontario as a powerful extratropical storm. Although the official hurricane season ended on November 15, a hurricane named Alice developed on December 30 to the northeast of the Lesser Antilles; it lasted until January 6 of the following year making the total for the year 11 tropical storms, 8 hurricanes, and 3 major hurricanes.

The 1955 Atlantic hurricane season eclipsed the devastation of 1954 with 13 storms. Alice, born in 1954, was the first, followed at a distance by Tropical Storm Brenda in August, which caused two deaths and some damage along the Gulf Coast of the United States. In the wake of Hurricanes Connie and Diane, Edith, Flora, Tropical Storm Five, and Hurricane Gladys caused a range of damage. Hurricane Hilda hit the Greater Antilles and then Mexico, followed by Hurricane Ione which struck eastern North Carolina causing seven fatalities and $88 million in damage. Hurricane Janet, which peaked as a Category 5 hurricane, followed, causing more than 700 deaths around the Caribbean Sea. A final tropical storm in October and Hurricane Katie capped off the season. (Other names held "in reserve" if the season had lasted longer included: Linda, Martha, Nelly, Orva, Peggy, Queena, Rosa, Stella, Trudy, Ursa, Verna, Wilma, Xenia, Yvonne, and Zelda!)

Now, for the first time since the early '60s, the Atlantic is back in an extended period of above average temperatures. Some predictions point to SST dropping back to average levels, or even below average as soon as 2015, but other interpretations point to a long period of above temperatures lasting well into the 2030s and perhaps even beyond, as SST increases due to global climate change. This is extremely alarming news, considering the possibility that global climate change could spur increased evaporation from the oceans *and* the melting of polar ice caps. The sudden release of huge volumes of freshwater from the poles could serve to drive up sea level and disrupt the salt concentration of seawater, thereby impairing thermohaline circulation and incurring much more dramatic AMO.

Our region faces an uncertain future. Hurricanes are no longer a question of if, but when. Perhaps the progeny of the Twisted Sisters will unleash wind, wave, and water upon an unprepared region once more.

—Eamon McCarthy Earls, 2014

Carol—August 31, 1954 – The First Sister's Visit

In August, 1954, New England newspaper readers learned of a perilous world that seemed to encroach on their peaceful preoccupations. In Europe, French Prime Minister Pierre Mendes France pushed to create a joint military to defend Western Europe against Soviet aggression, under an umbrella plan dubbed the European Defense Community. France was losing badly in Vietnam, with the final survivors of Ho Chi Minh's onslaught at the fort of Dien Bien Phu retreating with the help of the US. In addition to helping the French, the US 7th Fleet off of East Asia watched from the sidelines as the Nationalist and "Red" Chinese exchanged artillery fire and airstrikes across a string of disputed islands, while back in Washington, Senator Joe McCarthy rooted out suspected communists in government. Rhode Islanders, in particular, were scandalized to learn that the Stalin auto plant in Moscow had been found to use lathes and punch presses produced at the Abrasive Machine Tool Corp. in East Providence. The company president insisted the tools were sold under license before World War II, and that his company had had no dealings with the "Reds" since.

Fortunately, for New Englanders, the anxiety-inducing news reports of imminent conflict and war on all fronts could be put aside for a time. Other more mundane things filled the news. Upcoming elections gave the widely circulated *Providence Journal* plenty of local news to report. In North Kingstown, retired naval chief warrant officer Edward Neff was nominated for the state Senate, while the Warwick GOP tried to court women voters with three female candidates for local office. For tens of thousands of local women *not* pursuing political office, the newspaper had a different slate of advice. "Take your cumbersome home-making chores outdoors if you want to savor every minute of lovely late summer weather without falling behind in housework."

August was still part of the summer vacation season, and coastal communities throughout southern New England, from Saybrook, Connecticut to Cape Cod were flooded with vacationers. In Westerly, one of southern Rhode Island's busiest summer getaways, the month had started poorly due to, "cool weather and drizzly days." Bathhouse owners, concessions stands proprietors and parking lot managers prayed for the best. A reporter from the *Providence Journal* described their predicament, "The small businessmen at Westerly's numerous beaches—the guy who looks to the weatherman for his bread and butter—is crying as he watches the summer drift past his open door. The reason: Not one whopping Sunday crowd to make business a profitable pleasure."

While beach businesses toughed out the unseasonable weather, Rhode Islanders continued blithely through a summer free of serious storms. In fact, the first mention of a hurricane in August, 1954, did not refer to the deadly tropical weather systems at all. On August 6th, a used car business in Pawtucket posted a loud advertisement: "Hurricane warning! Dealers take shelter. YEP!—We're on rampage with an old fashioned Baker used car." The sort of storm that the Baker used car lot referred to was much different from the storm that they soon got.

By the end of the month, the first rumblings of a *real* storm came from the Weather Bureau. Alerts warned mariners of the threat posed by another Hurricane Carol, a new storm moving up the Eastern Seaboard, one that sported the same name as a modest hurricane that had brushed Maine in 1953. Because she was the third storm of the season, they had assigned her a name beginning with the third letter of the alphabet. "A strong possibility existed early today that the lash of hurricane Carol, which was off Cape Hatteras at midnight, may hit Rhode Island shores late today or early tonight," noted a news report. "A trough of low pressure which brought rain to this last night opened a path for the big storm to move in this direction. A condition very similar to that which preceded the 1938 hurricane," the report added.

However, Weather Bureau forecasters predicted conditions, "much less severe than the 1938 blow," with shoreline winds between 50 to 70 miles per hour (in Rhode Island) and approaching 50 to 60 miles per hour, northeasterly, by the early afternoon. A standard small craft advisory was issued, urging boaters to stay in harbor, and instructing larger ships to stay posted on changing conditions. At the Navy's massive Quonset Point Naval Air Station in North Kingstown, 71 propeller driven aircraft were flown inland to bases in Chicopee, Albany and Schenectady. Jet fighter planes—the cutting edge in 1954--were allowed to remain at the base because they were considered to be "all weather." However, pilots stood ready to fly them inland if conditions deteriorated.

The storm did not appear to concern many people initially, unless they were, themselves, small boat owners. Some of the nation's best amateur fishermen were arriving in the resort town of Narragansett, Rhode Island for the 12th Atlantic Tuna Tournament. Seventy-seven boats, representing 24 clubs and dozens of talented deep-water anglers had arrived in the small town, and were waiting anxiously to see how bad the weather would get. The captains agreed to put off a decision until the following morning at six a.m. One tournament official admitted, "Even under the worst conditions, some of them will still want to fish."

At sea, Hurricane Carol claimed its first victim in the Northeast. Forty-four year old Kurt Groteke, from the Bronx, died from exposure after floating in the icy, night waters of Long Island Sound. Groteke and his friend George Schuster, from Long Island, had boarded the cabin cruiser *Helen S.* and hurried for Block Island, trying to beat the storm. Instead, the boat capsized. By chance, William Lysinger, a deck officer on the destroyer escort *Raymond* noticed the orange life vests floating atop the dark waters of the sound and raised the alarm. Even though the *Raymond* and her sister ship *Nawman* carried out a swift rescue, they were unable to revive Groteke. Schuster was hospitalized in Newport when the two ships returned to their home base.

Early reports had also arrived from the Associated Press about the storm's impact further south. According to the Weather Bureau, hurricane force winds extended 100 miles to the east and 20 miles to the west of the storm's eye. Because the storm was expected to keep moving to the northeast from the Carolinas, hurricane warnings were put in effect from Manteo, North Carolina to Portsmouth, New Hampshire. The storm swept quickly through coastal North Carolina, washing away four piers at Wrightsville and Carolina Beach, breaking windows, flooding roads, and toppling trees and street signs. A roof was blown off a drill hall at the Marine Corps' huge base at Camp Lejeune. Tourists had been promptly evacuated from beach areas and returned to vacationing after eight p.m. Damage was light, but six natural disaster specialists were still dispatched from Washington by the Red Cross.

The Wilmington Weather Bureau office reported top wind speeds of 55 miles per hour, although forecaster Reuben Frost suggested 75-mile wind winds had raked local beaches. By 10 p.m., the storm was out to sea once again, 90 miles east of Wilmington, charting a course for Cape Hatteras by midnight. The winds were blowing 48 miles an hour with gusts reaching 60 miles per hour at Hatteras by 9:30 p.m.

A radio station in Savannah, Georgia intercepted a transmission from a ship offshore. Because the message was garbled, the ship's name did not come through, but what made it through was surprising. "Passed thru eye of Carol, northwest wind 125 miles per hour after eye passed. Carol has beautiful rainbow in her eye. Beach residents and island folk [must be] prepared for a hard blow." Then, New England went to sleep and the storm moved north, out of sight of land.

It wasn't to be a quiet sleep.

Two days later, on September 1st, the front page of regional newspapers told what had happened. Massive headline font announced the horrifying news to Rhode Island readers: "Hurricane leaves 16 dead, scores hurt, $100,000,000 damage along R.I. Coast."

The storm had slammed into the coast with unexpected ferocity. August 31st was a Tuesday, and the work week was in full swing. At Quonset Point, the Navy grew anxious about the weather at 9:30 in the morning, and evacuated the remaining jet fighters inland. Starting at 8:30 a.m. the Weather Bureau had warned of 'whole gale' force winds, but upgraded its alert to a definite hurricane warning at 10:30. A government meteorologist subsequently told reporters that he realized the 10:30 a.m. hurricane warning, "may have been a little late."

The warning truly was too little too late. The storm hit fifteen minutes later, reaching its peak intensity between 10:45 and 11:30 as workers watched fearfully from Providence office buildings.

The *Providence Journal*, Rhode Island's largest paper, was forced to temporarily relocate, and publish from the northern Rhode Island city of Woonsocket. Along with most of downtown Providence, the *Journal's* basement had flooded, "By 1:15 in the afternoon, Buell W. Hudson, the editor of the *Woonsocket Call*, was already offering *Journal* editors access to his presses." The *Fall River Herald-News* and the *Attleboro Sun* also temporarily relocated their operations to Woonsocket. Miraculously, the *Call's* office phones continued to work, and the newspaper helped to relay calls to Boston.

The raging waters sweeping into Providence did more than damage property. They claimed lives as well. Paul Hoye, a *Journal* correspondent employed his best paraphrasing to retell the harrowing story of Gaetase Gafio, a seven year old girl living on Pallas Street, in the hard hit Oakland Beach neighborhood.

"We were in the house, the three of us. We had been there since July. We were listening to the radio but there was no alarm. We weren't worried at first. Then the water

---

began to rise. The waves were high and pounding on the beach. My mother got hysterical. A fireman came by and told us he would check back later. Water had already surrounded the house by then. He never came back. About 9:30 the waves tore off the doors and windows on the first floor. My father and mother climbed to the second story. My mother was crying. My father was trying in vain to calm her."

"Slowly, the water began to mount to the second story. We were together in a bedroom. The water rose four feet in the bedroom. The house began to rock from side to side."

"Then I grew confused. I remember the house breaking apart and it getting dark. I went down under water, dazed and confused, but held my breath and kept bobbing up and down, trying to breathe. Then the walls backed open and the roof slid off to one side. Somehow I found an exit and got clear of the house. My parents had disappeared. As I slid clear, I caught hold of a large section of a wall or a roof. Clinging to that, and battered, beaten by debris, I hung on. I rode out the storm for about two hours. God was with me. Then I floated in towards shore where I was able to touch bottom and get help." The girl's parents were later listed among the dead.

A different reporter drew comparisons between Hurricane Carol and the fatal 1938 storm. "For Westerly it was 1938 all over again when yesterday's storm suddenly changed direction and piled a tidal wave along its coastline." Westerly, the South Coast's premier tourist destination was among the hardest hit communities, although damage was not, in the end, as severe as it had been during the 1938 hurricane, 16 years earlier.

Initially, the Westerly police reported only one person missing, a woman named Janet Rust, who had been staying in the Misquamicut area of town. The numbers began to grow. Before long, the Red Cross was reporting eight people missing, almost half the total number for the state. Three hundred cottages were destroyed, mostly in Misquamicut.

Elsewhere on the South Coast, the exclusive Watch Hill Beach Club was completely destroyed. Waves scoured the beaches in Charlestown and Quanachontaug, but no casualties were reported there. At Weekapaug, almost 40 "dune trailers" were washed away from a camp on the beach. In the afternoon, the Shore Road became one of the busiest routes in the state, with thousands of sightseers driving the route armed with binoculars. They peered curiously across Winnapaug, watching National Guard trucks and motorized skiffs rescuing stranded residents. In Westerly, the South Coast's gauge for storm severity was a pole with tidal marks showing the highest point reached by the 1938 and 1944 hurricane. Carol reached a point 19 inches below the other two storms.

In Providence, that Tuesday was one of the darkest nights in a long time, reminiscent of the eerie gloom of a wartime blackout. The Narragansett Electric Company's stations on South and Manchester Street were both flooded, and its system of underground wires and transformers used for importing outside electricity was soaked as well. Power was out in Newport and the Blackstone Valley Gas & Electric Company shutdown after the failure of a plant in Somerset. By a twist of fate the only place in the state with hope of speedy electrification was Westerly, perhaps thanks in part to the proximity of crews from Connecticut. Ultimately, 20 line crews from Massachusetts, New York and Pennsylvania were called in to help across the region.

During Carol's unannounced arrival in the city that morning, water levels along the Providence River, in the downtown rose dramatically and without warning. By noon, only an hour and 15 minutes after the start of hurricane conditions the downtown was submerged to an average depth of four feet—much deeper in some places. Office workers were stranded in their buildings, unable to navigate streets that had suddenly become swirling rivers. At the New England Telephone & Telegraph garage on Allens Avenue, the waters came in so fast that they nearly claimed the life of 63 year old Gaetano Lombardi, who was working in a locked office. A group of men heard his cries just in time. As it turned out, Lombardi was within minutes of drowning, as eight feet of water flooded into the garage.

The only company in the downtown that made it out unscathed was the United Transit Company, a bus company that had lost 20 "jitneys" during the 1938 storm. UTC hired private meteorologists at the Northeastern Weather Service in Lexington, Massachusetts when Carol was announced to avoid the mistakes of the '30s. This time they *were* prepared. At 6:49, an alert from Lexington told them that Carol would indeed be 'the big one.' UTC employees were sent to observe at the waterfront and phoned in when waters started to rise, giving bosses enough time to pull all company buses out of the downtown.

By evening, flood waters were slowly beginning to recede. In wrecked storefronts, hundreds of thousands of dollars of light fixtures and merchandise were ruined. National Guard troops poured into the city to protect businesses against looters. They followed the retreating waters as the sun crept from the sky. Firefighters tagged along, pumping water out of basements. Mayor Quigley took a different route to work than usual, riding in a small boat to City Hall. For the first time in several hours, the first floor was above water. He used a short-wave radio to contact city workers.

City drinking water supplies in East Providence were closed, and the Gulf Oil Company tank farm on the edge of the city was badly damaged. Meanwhile, hospitals were facing long lines and crowded wards, primarily due to injuries from flying glass. All grocery stores and restaurants in the downtown were closed until they could be re-inspected. Nevertheless, recovery had already begun. Drinking water was quickly declared safe, fuel tankers delivered at police and fire stations, and the all-important milkman resumed his route. Besides public safety buildings, the New England Telephone & Telegraph Company also remained open, welcoming unusually large crowds eager to make calls on the few telephones left in the city that still worked.

Some of the worst damage occurred along the Providence River, the narrow point where the stormy waters of the Narragansett Bay "funnel" were channeled. Nine cars in a parking lot on Dyer Street were 'totaled.' In fact, one of the cars was flipped on its roof. The others were buried hub deep in river sand. Water remained eight feet above street level on South Water and India Street.

With the exception of Rhode Island companies that had actually sustained damage from flooding or falling trees, business was booming in the aftermath of the storms. For some Providence folk, the storm was a blessing in disguise. "Small diners, in high sections above the water damage, did thriving business around dinner time...[and] A few enterprising shoestring businessmen found unexpected prosperity," according to a news report. One of those entrepreneurs was an old man, who claimed his name was "Lucky," selling 20 cent candles to pedestrians on Westminster Street.

"Whether it was a diner, a hardware store, a lumber yard, or a five and dime, Rhode Island merchants, especially in shore areas did a business that has been equaled only by the day after the 1938 hurricane," noted a reporter. Most hardware stores were stripped clean of coal within 15 minutes of restock. Kerosene, axes, flashlights, roofing paper and shingles were in high demand, but according to shop keepers, window glass was less in demand than in 1938. One hardware store owner bemoaned his recent "fall cleanup," because he had returned a number of camp stoves, leaving him with only four in stock at the time of the storm. Restaurants too were packed, as food began to mold in refrigerators. One South County establishment threatened to close unless customers came behind the counter to help out.

Insurance firms did not enjoy Carol any more than they enjoyed the subsequent 1950s New England hurricanes. The Providence Washington Insurance Company issued its first payment at 10:30, the morning after the storm. Switchboards were "swamped," as a first round of 3,000 claims came in. A hundred stock insurance companies pooled their efforts through the General Adjustment Bureau, sending in 100 adjustors from the South and the Mid-West. The Mutual Fire Insurance Association of New England moved its "catastrophe office" from Boston to temporary quarters in Mutual Place in Providence, to deal with the inevitable claims to be made by 100,000 policy holders in the area.

In fact, insurance companies breathed a sigh of relief that one aspect of recovery was less challenging. In the 10 years after the end of World War II, thousands of Rhode Island families had flocked to nearby suburban communities at the periphery of large Ocean State cities. These new homes often had outdoor fireplaces and camp stoves, which were very adaptable to cooking without regular utilities. These new homeowners prized green lawns and often had tanks of gasoline lying around for their lawnmowers, taking some of the burden off of gas stations.

The storm also impacted farmers and federal workers. The Providence Post Office flooded with 15 feet of water (reduced to four feet with pumping the following day) lost four million dollars in waterlogged stamps. The Internal Revenue Service—every resident's favorite agency—was fortuitously closed. Eight feet of water had floated 20 desks, sending them crashing through a plate glass window, throwing soggy returns all over the office. Twenty million dollars of stored Federal Reserve depository receipts were "inundated" as well.

In rural Rhode Island 80 different dairy operations were forced to dump thousands of gallons of milk, each. East Greenwich Dairy alone dumped 6,000, and hoped that it would be able to send future shipments to Massachusetts. The same dairy farm lost a truck which became completely buried beneath a new sand dune. The day after the storm was the first in many years for older farmers, and the first time *ever* for young farmers, to milk their herds by hand. No power meant no access to milking machines. Others decided not to return to the old ways and simply paid the extra money to import milk from Connecticut.

Crop growers suffered serious losses in orchards. Tractors were used to pull trees back into a standing position, while harvesters were hurried into the orchards to pick whatever apples had survived. Tomato and grape crops were beaten badly, and in South County, gallon after gallon of briny seawater browned clover and alfalfa. Fortunately, the ubiquitous Rhode Island Reds at poultry farms kept laying and putting on weight.

By September 7, Rhode Island was beginning to return to normalcy. "Downtown Providence was jolted back to life a few hours before dawn yesterday with a terrific surge of electric power." According to the *Providence Journal*, Ninety percent of homes had power and telephone service back, and thousands of Ocean State employees were returning to work.

Carol remained destructive, but presented a "soft shoulder" to Connecticut. Only one death was reported, that of 55 year old Herman Zarnestke in New Haven. However, Zarnetske's death was not strictly attributable to the storm, resulting from a fatal heart attack.

On August 28, even as neighboring Rhode Islanders and Massachusetts residents carried on with everyday business, Hartford was preoccupied with business that seemed particularly mundane. The leading issue in the city's print news media was a debate in the Public Utilities Commission about whether or not bus drivers should issue receipts to riders. The commission finally agreed that receipts could be issued, but only by special request from a rider. State Police Commissioner Kelly demanded that the state legislature fund newer, more "efficient" (read: faster) police cruisers needed, "as soon as the new cross-state expressway is completed."

On September 1st, the *Hartford Courant* offered less front-page coverage to its readers, but more coverage overall, with an itemized list of the storm's impact in every major town and city in the state. "A hurricane, dying but still deadly, swept across Connecticut Tuesday, felling trees and wires, ravaging crops and flooding the shoreline." Tides rose swiftly along the coast, catching vacationers in their cottages by surprise. Great Hammocks in Old Saybrook was hardest hit with seven cottages destroyed. Twenty five people had to be rescued by the Essex Fire Department's war surplus DUKW "Duck" amphibious truck. Three National Guard units were deployed to prevent looting along the shoreline. The Weather Bureau office at Bradley Field reported maximum winds of 64 miles per hour, 24 minutes past noon.

Out a sea, a group of Connecticut Girl Scouts rode out the storm aboard the schooner, *Brilliant*. The eight girls and their troop leader were caught in the storm at Shelter Island, just off of Long Island. Even with three anchors out and the engine running, the schooner was being pushed closer and closer to Shelter Island Yacht Club. Within 50 feet of the shore, the girls were ordered to come up from below decks, and don life vests before they were rowed to the wharf. The wharf was flooded and all of the Scouts were immediately soaked. The club members were very welcoming and offered them hot coffee which helped to make the cold, soaking clothes bearable for a little bit. But when storm waters raged through the clubhouse door, submerging the room in two feet of water, the girls were called upon to help lug furniture to safety. Ultimately, the schooner was saved, and the girls were able to continue their cruise the following day.

Like their neighbors in Massachusetts and Rhode Island, growers were unhappy about the storm. MacIntosh apples, the state's most valuable crop, were caught just 10 days before harvest. Around one-third of the shade tobacco that had not been picked by savvy farmers before the storm lay flattened in the mud. Corn stalks, although twisted, remained standing in most fields, and peaches were spared the worst—late season peaches were still hard as rocks, maturing on their branches. Two days after the storm, professors at the University of Connecticut in Storrs put their services at the disposal of farmers and homeowners, to give any kind of advice needed to handle ailing crops or battered roofs.

New Britain was one of several large communities that lost power and telephone service. Within the city, 9,000 telephone customers had no service. Plate glass windows broke throughout the downtown, and a crack nearly cleaved the smokestack at the American Hardware Corporation plant. In Winsted, fire alarms were knocked out, giving firefighters little advanced warning of a blaze at the Brown Machine Company. The panicked fire captain finally marshaled his company making full use of both short-wave radio and the local telephone switchboard.

However, Carol's reach was not restricted to Connecticut and Rhode Island. The storm inflicted heavy damage in parts of eastern Massachusetts and more limited damage in southern New Hampshire and Maine; Vermont remained largely untouched.

The damage estimates from September 1st, a day after the storm, indicated 35 people dead in Long Island and New England, and *higher* property damage than that inflicted by the Hurricane of '38. The New England Telephone & Telegraph Company announced 2.5 million feet of telephone lines torn down from their poles, and serious fire hazards in woodland areas (state parks in particular) where thousands of toppled trees had become a new source of kindling for forest fires.

Within Massachusetts half of the apple and corn crops were ruined. Total farm losses ran as high as five million dollars. The number also included tobacco losses which were comparatively light—only 20 percent of the crop—because most of the state's tobacco farms were located in Western Massachusetts. Looting soon broke out in Salem and in parts of Cape Cod. Martial law was declared in Bourne, on Cape Cod, and in Malden, north of Boston, and the National Guard was ordered to patrol the streets in Newburyport.

Around Massachusetts Bay, Boston and Revere each suffered a million dollars in damage. The Old North Church, a historic landmark, and site of the famous signal that launched Paul Revere's call to arms, was badly damaged. Part of the steeple splintered, leaving the spire leaning crazily over the street below. Along Soldiers Field Road in

Brighton, the new WBZ-TV broadcasting tower blew over, narrowly missing the studio itself.

New Bedford, the largest city in southeastern Massachusetts may have had the worst experience with Carol of any place in Massachusetts. Damage totals exceeded 50 million dollars, (slightly less than half a billion in 2014 dollars). The area was, "battered and dazed by the blow," which left 10 dead in greater New Bedford. Property damage was actually worse with Carol than with the no-name storm of 1938. A state of "semi-martial law" existed throughout New Bedford, as well as the neighboring towns of Fairhaven, South Dartmouth, and Mattapoisett, according to the *Boston Post*.

High winds drove seawater several hundred feet inland, quickly racking up $10 million in damage to coastal factories. The tide was 10.5 feet above average, reaching points that 1938 had left high and dry. Frighteningly, the storm's abrupt arrival and sudden fury lasted only two hours.

Mayor Harriman swiftly held an emergency meeting to appropriate $400,000 for an emergency clean-up fund. From all across the eastern United States, emergency crews trickled in. Telephone crews arrived from close by places such as Quincy and Western Massachusetts to restore 5,000 lines, but power crews also arrived from much farther afield: Pennsylvania, New York, Boston, and Orleans, Massachusetts. To the east of New Bedford, from Westport to the start of Cape Cod in Wareham, coastal homes were gutted and destroyed.

Although the acute damage to local industry made up only one-fifth of overall damage totals, it may have been the most significant. Major employers such as Aerovox (which employed 3,000 people and incurred two million dollars damage), Acushnet Processing, Wamsutta Mills, Fairhaven Mills, and Revere Copper and Brass closed due to flooding. Corporate insurance policies covered wind damage, but not damage from the tidal surge. The storm came at a bad time. "New Bedford industries already suffering from a lack of orders and unemployment, received a stunning blow..." announced the *New Bedford Standard-Times.* Many of the city's workers were employed by large mills, but the city was buttressed by a second major industry: fishing. But with a large portion of boats sunk, or damaged in the harbor, even the fishing industry was reeling.

Three days after Carol, *New Bedford Standard-Times* staff photographer, Hal Nielson was sent aloft in a small plane to take aerial photos of the changes along the South Coast. In 1938, Nielson had flown a similar mission, and what he saw this time horrified him. "I'll say it looked bad—the housing damage, that is—than what I saw [in] 1938..." He added, "Swifts Beach, Wareham, and East Beach, Horseneck, are the scenes of desolation that stand out most sharply...You could almost shoot blindfolded, over Swifts Beach and get a disaster scene. Wrecked houses, uprooted and splintered trees covered our field of vision." Few locations stood out as much as East Beach at Horseneck, which was, "swept so clean a picture of the beach alone couldn't tell the story." In fact, Nielson took a wider view to show how far the houses—what remained of them—had been tossed.

Mattapoisett's wharves proved startling. Nielson almost skipped taking pictures because the wharves were so clear of debris. But then he noticed something unusual; the buildings that once stood on the wharves had completely disappeared. "It was just as if someone had taken a huge broom and swept them off. Anyone unfamiliar with the spot wouldn't have known anything was wrong."

Off of Cape Cod, Martha's Vineyard appeared much like the rest of the South Coast. The good news according to the state police, was that no lives were lost, no fires had broken out, and in fact, nobody was seriously injured on the island. Nonetheless, Carol inflicted millions in damage to the Vineyard, with 75-mile per hour sustained winds recorded at the airport in the center of the island. Highways along the beach were washed out, and cottages were ruined along with private and commercial boats. When he flew over the island, Nielson remarked that Martha's Vineyard was, "fortunate" compared with the mainland. Many boats had washed ashore, and one or two homes lacked roofs, but otherwise the only sign of trouble from the air, was the larger than normal crowd of cars lining up for the ferry.

To the north, Carol struck New Hampshire and Maine similarly. Three people were killed by the storm, and a fourth indirect fatality came a day after the storm when 45 year old, Frank Horton died of a heart attack while clearing downed branches in Plaistow. Although property damage was widespread, it was not severe enough for New Hampshire to qualify for federal aid. Orchards lost $1.5 million. Clement Lyon, head of the Division of Market and Standards told reporters that between 50 and 90 percent of MacIntosh apples growing in Merrimack and Hillsborough County were on the ground. Reports from Seacoast growers were slow to come in because of fallen telephone lines.

Maine suffered eight serious casualties of the storm. Portland resident Robert Cormier was crushed by a falling tree while he was shopping in a store on the city's Brighton Avenue. Bancroft Bealey was washed off the deck of a yawl offshore and drowned, while a 60-year old woman from New Brunswick was killed in a car crash in Columbia Falls, in the eastern part of the state. Offshore, a 38-foot sloop *Katahdin*, owned by the Hutchinson family went missing. In addition to the adults onboard, their two children, and a third young passenger were also sought by rescuers. The vice-president of the Central Maine Power Company termed the storm the worst since the hurricane of '38. It left towns and cities along the coast nearly abandoned as factories sent their workers home. At Portland's Yacht Club, and a similar marina in Camden, bystanders watched anxiously as heavy seas reduced luxury yachts to matchwood.

The storm did produce at least one positive result. "...this one did blow some good. A public smorgasbord supper designed to raise funds for the emergency polio March of Dimes was mobbed." The charity dinner received a hefty crowd, and hefty donations to aid the ongoing fight against polio.

Oxford County in southwestern Maine, bordering New Hampshire was particularly impacted. Carol hit the "Twin Towns" of Norway and South Paris, snapping and splintering "scores" of trees which blocked Main Street and the main roads leading into the community. Industrial workers were sent home at two p.m. after falling branches from

100-year old trees tore down nearly every high tension wire, shutting off power to homes and factories. National Guardsmen and highway workers set about clearing the streets with powerful chainsaws. The Twin Towns considered themselves fortunate that nobody was hurt, although the storm did incur one written-off vehicle. A sixty foot elm tree snapped eight feet above the ground and crashed down on the front of a truck, owned by South Paris motorist Velko Havrinen. He had parked the truck at the Market Square Shell station to put new tires on it. The upper branches of the elm scuffed up a pickup truck, but Harold Johnson, the station's mechanic breathed a sigh of relief—he was rolling tires toward the truck at the moment the tree fell.

On the other side of town, Eunice Barrows was celebrating her 90th birthday the day of the storm. Her neighbor, Marguerite Shaw pulled up in her car, parking outside the Barrows home for a birthday visit. Barrows' son-in-law, Reverend Milton McAllister could foresee a bad outcome, because Shaw's car was parked close to an old tree growing in the yard. At his suggestion she moved her car, just in time. The tree fell moments later.

Three quarters of the shipbuilding community of Bath was plunged into darkness. Simultaneously, branches tore down New England Telephone & Telegraph lines, cutting off phone service. Bath Iron Works and Hyde Windlass Company—two of the city's largest employers—shut down in the afternoon as a result of the outage, but the Central Maine Power Company managed to keep the lights on in Bath Memorial Hospital and the pumping station. Nearby Brunswick greeted the storm differently. "One would have thought they were on a picnic," noted one observer. "Fathers, mothers, brothers, sisters, people of all ages walking or driving through the streets to see what the damage was. The fact that branches and limbs and wires were falling all around them did not faze the excitement seekers in the least."

In fact, the "excitement seekers" created an even bigger mess for police and Civil Defense volunteers trying to clear the roads of branches to allow emergency vehicles to pass, snarling the streets with traffic. In the words of the *Portland Press Herald*, "They circled endlessly from one end of town to another, gawking at the damage." Power was shut off as the number of fallen wires climbed, to prevent accidental electrocution of passersby. Brunswick Town Manager Merle Goff guessed that the clean-up would cost the town $5,000 and homeowners several thousand dollars more to fix damaged roofs. Officers at the naval air station located in the town, dispatched teams with chain saws to help clear broken branches; during the storm many of their ground crews stayed on alert for long periods, keeping an eye on planes lashed to the tarmac.

South Freeport, Brunswick's southern neighbor and the present day home of L.L. Bean, nearly lost the South Freeport Boat Company's wharf. Laurent Lunt, the police chief, reported many trees down like other towns to the north and west. Local officials and reporters concluded that the worst hit towns in southern Maine were North Bridgton, Casco, and Naples, although South Paris, Norway, South Freeport, Brunswick and Bath were not far behind. The power of nature was on full display outside of Bridgton Academy in North Bridgton, where 35 elm trees either snapped, or leaned—roots exposed—out of the soft earth. Boaters were far from pleased to discover 50 smashed pleasure boats in North Sebago, on the shores of Sebago Lake.

Perhaps hardest hit of all were the state's apple growers. Governor Burton Cross wired President Eisenhower to ask for an emergency cash grant to tide over farmers, whose orchards experienced two million dollar losses. The State Agriculture Department agreed to allow farmers to sell their numerous drop-apples, so long as they were properly labelled. Work crews yearned for sleep, but kept working to bring back power by the following Monday, while families switched to candles, ice pails, and canned food for their light and food storage needs. The situation was inconvenient, but the state had been spared the worst of the storm.

However, normalcy would have to wait. A new storm—dubbed Hurricane Edna— was heading out to sea, and coming north on a collision course with New England.

Cruel Carol

Massive waves crash into the second story of homes in Old Lyme, Connecticut. Coastal Connecticut witnessed tides eight feet higher than usual. (Courtesy NOAA)

Carol's storm surge inundates the Rhode Island Yacht Club, a popular local landmark severely damaged in the storm. (Courtesy NOAA)

An aerial photograph of Westerly, Rhode Island reveals the extent of storm damage. Note the ranch houses in the center of image thrown off their foundations. (Courtesy National Guard)

Carol's storm surge rips into a neighborhood at an unidentified location along the southern New England coast.

Shown in this aerial photograph is a roofless home at the end of Misquamicut Beach in Westerly. (Courtesy National Guard)

A ruined sailboat in Marblehead harbor. (Courtesy Boston Public Library)

The car in the center of the image has seen better days as a fallen oak tree slowly crushes its roof. (Courtesy Boston Public Library)

Groups of local men roam the beach (left) and seawall (right) inspecting ruined boats, debris, and large logs cast up on shore in Marblehead. (Courtesy Boston Public Library)

This uprooted tree in the park looks as if it has taken a few park benches with it. The Mass. Trades Shop School, at left, was based in Boston. (Courtesy Boston Public Library)

These men inspect a sailboat and two cabin cruisers blown onto the beach. Wooden boats such as these were easily destroyed in hurricane force winds, but these boats appear to have survived the worst of Carol's fury. (Courtesy Boston Public Library)

Barrels and newly-minted driftwood bob gently alongside small sailboats in what may be Marblehead harbor. (Courtesy Boston Public Library)

Tugboats, freighters and fishing boats rafted onto the shore in Fairhaven harbor (Courtesy New Bedford Whaling Museum)

A car parks by the bow of a trawler driven against the side of a warehouse in Fairhaven harbor (Courtesy New Bedford Whaling Museum)

A tugboat settles onto the bottom next to a wharf in Fairhaven harbor. The gutted back (upper left) reads Lackawanna Railroad on the side. (Courtesy New Bedford Whaling Museum)

The *Whaling City* out of New York lists uncomfortably onshore in Fairhaven harbor. Note the splintering of ship's wooden hull. (Courtesy New Bedford Whaling Museum)

Hurricane Carol - 1954
Rainfall 2 inches or greater

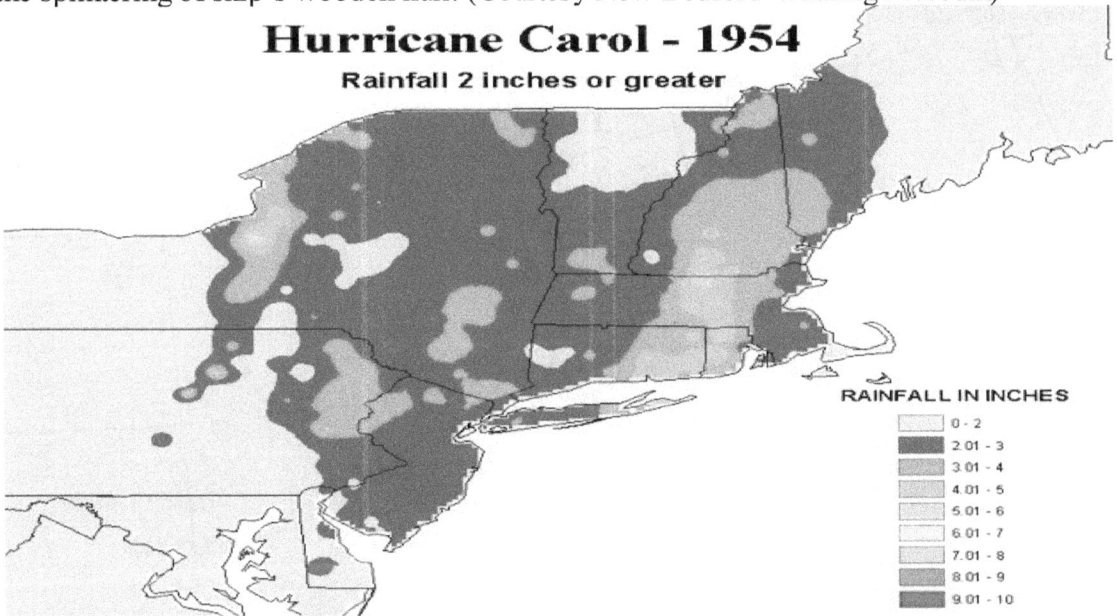

RAINFALL IN INCHES

	0 - 2
	2.01 - 3
	3.01 - 4
	4.01 - 5
	5.01 - 6
	6.01 - 7
	7.01 - 8
	8.01 - 9
	9.01 - 10

Although much of Carol's damage was dealt by winds and the coastal storm surge, the hurricane was also a major rain event throughout the Northeast, dropping large volumes of water across a wide area. Rhode Island, north-central Massachusetts, and western New York witnessed some of the most intense rains.

ADVISORY POSITIONS-HURRICANE "EDNA"

1	5:00pm	Sept 6	22.3N	70.7W
2	11:00pm	6	22.3N	71.5W
3	5:00am	7	22.5N	72.2W
4	11:00am	7	23.3N	73.3W
5	5:00pm	7	23.9N	74.2W
6	11:00pm	7	24.8N	74.8W
7	5:00am	8	25.3N	75.3W
8	11:00am	8	26.0N	75.7W
9	5:00pm	8	26.8N	75.6W
10	11:00pm	8	27.5N	75.6W
11	5:00am	9	28.4N	75.8W
12	11:00am	9	28.6N	76.6W
13	5:00pm	9	29.1N	76.4W
14	11:00am	9	30.3N	76.2W
15	5:00am	10	31.0N	76.1W
16	11:00am	10	31.8N	75.6W
17	5:00pm	10	34.0N	75.3W
18	11:00pm	10	35.5N	74.1W
19	5:00am	11	37.7N	73.1W
20	11:00am	11	40.0N	71.0W
21	5:00pm	11	43.0N	69.0W
22	11:00pm	11	46.0N	66.0W

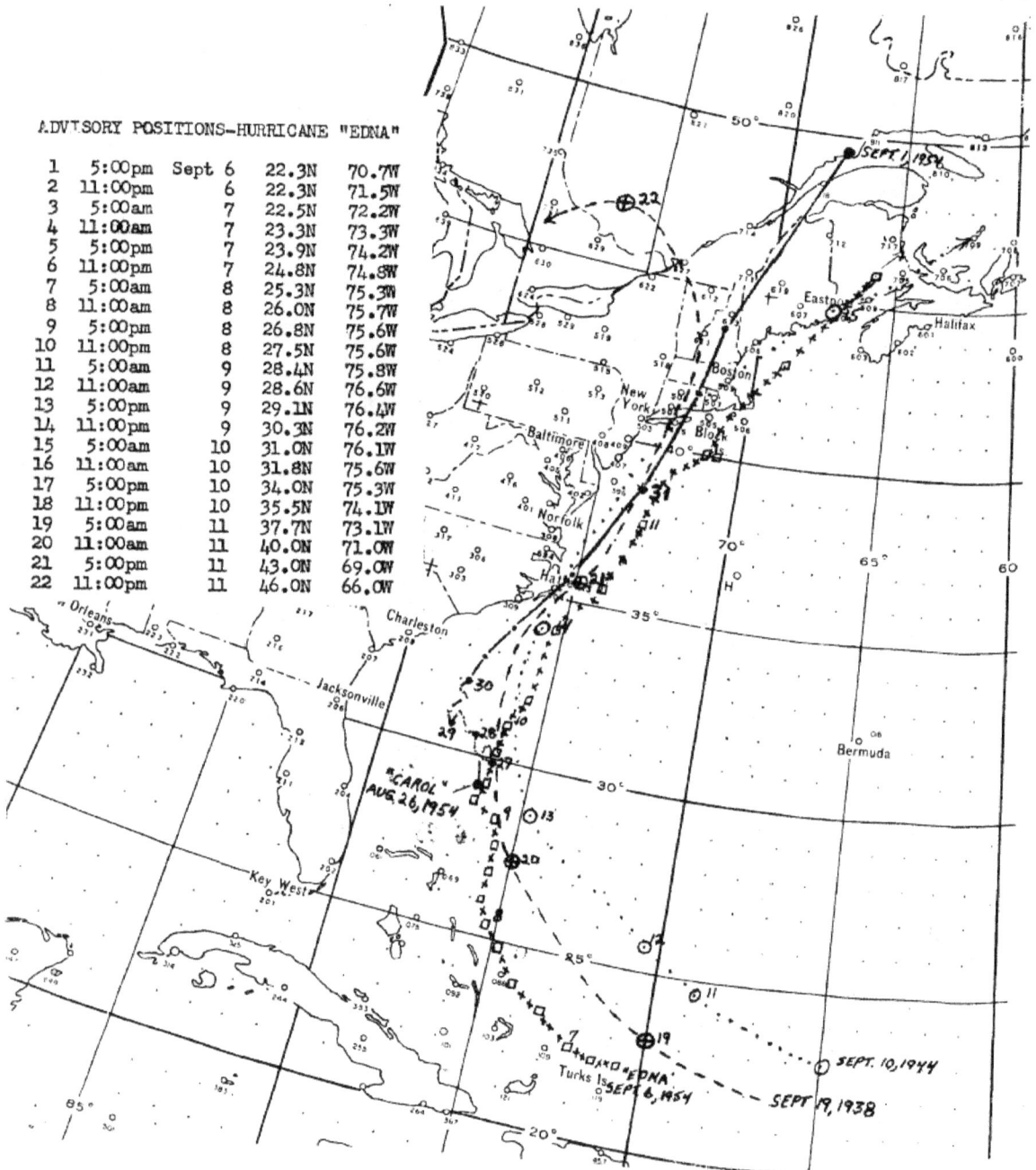

Marked with a diamond-X pattern, this Weather Bureau map records the path of Hurricane Edna from the Turks & Caicos Islands to Eastport, Maine and New Brunswick. The storm made landfall in New England on September 11, 1954, little more than a week after Hurricane Carol.

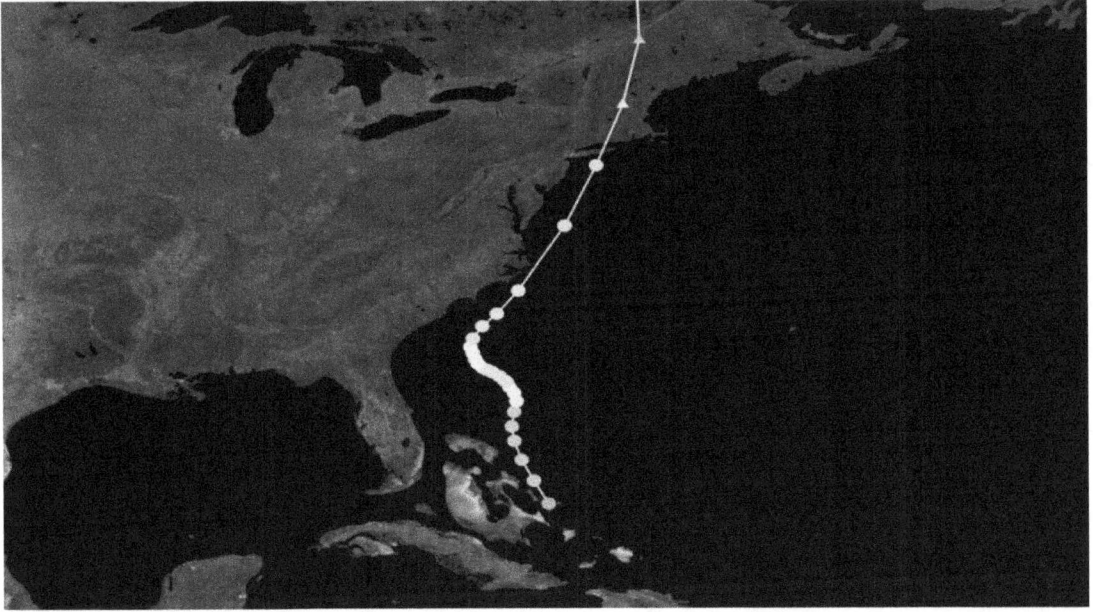

The track of Hurricane Carol is shown here on a modern satellite map of the east coast.

Edna—September 11, 1954—The Second Sister

Connecticut had braced for the possibility of a storm stronger than Carol, that might hit the state more directly herself. At five o'clock in the afternoon on Monday, September 6, 1954, the Miami field office of the Weather Bureau spotted a storm system brewing off of the Florida coast. Sixty miles to the northeast of the Turks & Caicos Islands in the southern Bahamas chain, a tropical storm was forming from an easterly wave. The Weather Bureau issued an "Advisory No. 1" alerting meteorologists and mariners along the Eastern Seaboard about the budding weather system, dubbed Hurricane Edna.

Alarming statements by assistant meteorologist James Osmun, who announced that, "it will be a miracle if Edna does not hit New York City head-on tomorrow," helped Civil Defense officials to rise to the occasion. An observer noted, "Tension gripped the coast from Cape Hatteras to Maine. For Edna—the season's fifth Atlantic hurricane and named after the fifth letter of the alphabet—aptly bore a woman's name. She maintained the prerogative of changing her mind." The American Automobile Association urged motorists to stay off of the roads between Washington, DC and Connecticut.

In Hartford, Mayor DeLuco mobilized Civil Defense workers, and prepared $100,000 in storm aid. Bulldozers cleared a patch of land to receive (and presumably incinerate) storm debris, while WKNB-TV set up a direct line to the Weather Bureau. Vacationers boarded up their cottages, and line crews stood at the ready. The state development commission issued canvas tarpaulins and sandbags to coastal factories. State police patrols were assigned a stretch of coastline between Old Lyme and Clinton lacking a local police force of its own. Governor John Davis Lodge told citizens that air raid sirens would be sounded in three minute intervals as an "all clear" once the storm had passed. He would spend the storm at a forward base at Camp Lodge, in Niantic, with his aides.

Phone workers were also mobilized. All switchboard operators were called in along with the full force of 3,000 linemen who conducted patrols through the state and manned 11 substations that were usually left unattended. One North Coventry milkman, William McKinney, surprised his customers by showing up a day early with their deliveries. When asked to explain his earlier than usual run, McKinney replied, "Too many babies in the area. I worried too much during the last hurricane about them. Now, if the storm hits, I won't have to start worrying until Monday, my next delivery date."

Edna picked up speed as she departed the warm waters at the edge of the Caribbean Sea, following 'hot on the heels' of Carol 11 days earlier. Her wind speeds varied between 75 and 125 miles per hour off of Cape Hatteras in North Carolina. Weather Bureau officials in Miami were comforted to see the storm behaving less unpredictably than Carol. When the storm was first detected, it was traveling at a fairly sedate six miles per hour to the northwest. A day later, on September 7th, Edna had picked up speed, doubling its pace. Over the next two days, the storm hovered between eight and 10 miles per hour. By September 10th, as Edna neared Cape Hatteras in the North Carolina, her horizontal progress over the gray-green North Atlantic increased once again. By 11 p.m. meteorologists were tracking movement of as much as 25 miles per hour.

Edna's acceleration up the Eastern Seaboard was not unexpected, but the storm's twin eyes were certainly not anticipated. On Saturday, September 11th, the storm reached 40 miles per hour, moving over Martha's Vineyard at 1:45 p.m. By 7:30 p.m. the storm was striking Eastport, Maine before heading over the Gulf of Maine. Fifteen minutes after the storm made landfall in Martha's Vineyard, radar revealed two eyes, approximately 60 miles apart and each rotating counterclockwise around one another.

"[It] would certainly give a confused picture of...[the storm's] position and path." The Weather Bureau was not able to conclusively prove that the storm had shown the twin-eyed pattern throughout its movement up the East Coast, but the Bureau acknowledged that the eyes may have shifted within the storm, bringing one or the other closer to the land. The radar discovery helped to clear up some confusing readings that the Weather Bureau had amassed as they tracked the storm. Between Cape Hatteras and Nantucket, radar operators and airborne storm reconnaissance teams had placed the storm in different locations.

Famed CBS journalist Edward R. Murrow took readers into the storm with his transcribed account of riding into Edna aboard a B-29 bomber converted for the Air Weather Service. "Although every control was set to take us down, something lifted us up about 300 feet. Then the pilot said, 'we're going down,' although he was doing everything possible to take us up. Edna was in control of the aircraft."

"We were on an even keel but being staggered by short, sharp blows. Then we hit something with a bang that was audible above the roar of the motors—a solid sheet of water. Seconds later, brilliant sunshine hit us like a hammer: someone shouted, 'there she is,' and we were in the eye."

"Calm air, flat, calm sea, below; a great amphitheater....round as a dollar, with white clouds sloping up to 25 to 30 thousand feet..."

"Someone, I thin[k] it was me, there's a ship down there' and there's a ship down there,' and there was—right in the center of the eye. We guessed her to be a 10,000 ton merchant ship, moving very slowly in that calm water...she appeared to be in no trouble, but trouble was inevitable sometime, because she was surrounded by those cloud mountains and raging water."

As it turns out, Hurricane Edna was mostly a close call for five of the New England states. Out of six New England states, Edna's impact was felt most heavily in Maine and, in fact, remains the most expensive storm to ever hit the Pine Tree State. The state experienced the heaviest rainfall since 1896—a span of 58 years. The state was temporarily isolated from the rest of New England as roads, bridges and railroads were swept away. Damage from washouts was so extensive that Civil Defense officials were hard pressed to count the number of roads that had been cut.

The storm swept up the coast, "...grazing the populous northeast in a breathtaking near-miss." Winds up to 95 miles per hour were recorded at Brookhaven National Laboratory on Long Island, virtually on New England's doorstep. The storm raced out to sea once again, crossing the Gulf of Maine, and inflicting heavy damage in the Bay of Fundy and southern Nova Scotia.

All told, Edna left 11 people dead, including five in New England. The majority of Edna's casualties were drivers who wrecked in the heavy rainfall and high winds, although one man was electrocuted by a downed power line, and two people in Maine drowned.

In Rhode Island, Edna's arrival was greeted with both anxiety and an eventual sigh of relief. Edna was far less damaging than Carol. "A merciful Hurricane Edna yesterday slapped Rhode Island with a backlash of vicious northwest winds, but spared the groggy state the devastation of its worst winds and seas." Lights remained on in Providence, although they did blink out in neighboring communities. All downtown stores remained closed, with guardsmen sandbagging the street. The downtown was a virtual ghost town, populated with a few emergency workers and 10 hardened movie goers, watching *Dragnet* in a theater.

Three and a half inches of rain fell across the state. What little damaged occurred seemed to be concentrated in Newport. There, the Sunday after the storm was scheduled as a time to collect hurricane debris. Public works trucks would patrol the city, picking up debris placed on walkways for six in the morning. City manager, William Gildea, announced that the solution to the "almost never ending challenge," would come from residents, who, he hoped, would help to load city trucks. Trucks had already been forced to visit the same neighborhoods as much as four times because residents had not been ready to throw out debris.

In Salem, Massachusetts, the September 11th storm nearly brought an end to 12 young lives. Three nurses and 12 babies ranging in age from one month to three years old were hurriedly evacuated in police cruisers. The nurses had sat down to dinner, when a 70 foot tall chimney, rising above the hospital leaned and toppled on the roof over their heads, showering the operating room and the nurse's break room with bricks. Miraculously, no one was hurt, even though the chimney crushed the table where the nurses had been sitting. Edna's heavy rains came pouring in through the roof, drenching the building so extensively that the staff expected it to flood. It was later concluded that the chimney had been previously weakened by Hurricane Carol.

Elsewhere on the North Shore, Edna's winds wrecked the historic Topsfield fairground, ripping the roof off of the Greyhound Racing Association club.

The storm was somewhat unusual, with two "eyes" instead of the usual central eye typically seen in most hurricanes. One eye of the storm passed over Bar Harbor, Maine while its associate swept over Bangor. In near total blackness as the city labored under a power outage, Maine's Civil Defense volunteer mobilized in Bangor in an effort to evacuate residents from low-lying areas surrounding the Penobscot River,

However, the Weather Bureau did note some good news that came out of Edna. The storm had been much less destructive than anticipated, due, ironically, to Hurricane Carol. The devastation and damage left behind by Carol was only just beginning to be cleaned up when Edna arrived. But Carol had sent a clear message: a New England hurricane was not something to be trifled with. Unlike Carol, the storm produced fairly limited damage in New Jersey and New York's Long Island. People throughout the Northeast were warned rapidly by radio, TV and newspapers about the hurricane alert, and bearing the lessons of Carol in mind, many people evacuated or took precautions.

Because Carol's high winds had coincided with high tide, the storm drove large amounts of seawater ashore in a terrifying storm surge. Edna, on the other hand, dumped huge quantities of rain water, except in Montauk Point, New York, where a fresh storm surge caused damage. The storm actually covered a larger area than Carol, but generated similar gusts. Meteorologists at the Bureau's 17 Battery Place office, in New York City, logged peak gusts of 61 miles per hour in each storm, even though Edna was actually traveling farther to the east than Carol. The storm reached its height between 6 a.m. on September 11, for another 14 long hours, until 9 p.m. High intensity, gale force winds were noted during each of the 14 hours of the storm's peak, lasting far longer than the six hours of high winds that accompanied Carol.

A recurring theme in the 1950s New England hurricanes is the question of the local milk supply, which was a crucial concern at a time when most customers still received their milk fresh from nearby farms in reusable glass bottles, as a daily delivery. As McKinney, the North Coventry milkman's urgency suggests, dairy milk was the main source of sustenance for thousands of cradle-dwelling 'baby boomers.' The introduction of powdered baby food and other elixirs for the modern mother had turned breastfeeding into an old-fashioned activity, leaving babies less disaster resistant.

A particularly amusing storm story arrived from New London. "*New London Day* Reporter Deane C. Avery was pounding out his Hurricane Edna story today when the telephone rang. He listened a moment and then exclaimed."

'It's happened!'

'What,' queried a fellow reporter?

'My wife just had twins, a boy and a girl,' shouted Avery.

'Congratulations,' beamed the fellow reporter. 'Name them Edna and Edward."

Recovery work for Rhode Island included rebuilding an infrastructural trifecta on the Barrington River. "Two score" men, from three different work crews, converged to rebuild a washed out rail bridge and causeway, as well as five high tension power lines. The group included linemen from New England Light Company and Western Union Telegraph Company, but the largest crew was from the New York, New Haven & Hartford Railroad.

South Easton Pond and Nonquit Pond in Tiverton both served as public water supplies for Newport, and each had to be drained because of heavy salt content from the twin storms. Fifty thousand dollars in damage had occurred at the Paradise Avenue pumping station, and the building had to be "electrically dried" to prevent any more damage to the submerged motors. The water commissioner was grateful that the storms had arrived when they did, because of the upcoming fall rainy season that would help to flush the ponds even further. Woonsocket residents took some reassuring that their water supply was, in fact, safe. Tap water had taken on a brownish tinge after leaves were stirred up by the storms. Adequately chlorinated, it was safe to drink, but the lack of a sand filter to clear the water made it look quite unappealing.

Further north, Maine had braced for the worst. Although Hurricane Edna had weakened, it continued to pose a very real threat to the state, racing northward with winds that came close to 100 miles per hour. Civil Defense personnel and state staff members set up alert centers in eight counties: Lincoln, Knox, Hancock, Cumberland, Sagadahoc, Waldo, Washington and York. Rescue trucks were dispatched to Orono and Scarboro, while others were sent to collect four generators from Fort Devens in Massachusetts.

By seven in the morning, Maine's state government was ready for anything. Last minute updates went out to readers and listeners through AP and UP news wires. Governor Cross ordered churches, schools and public buildings in coastal areas to open as emergency shelters. Throughout the morning reports flooded in from Civil Defense centers and 16 Forestry Department mobile communication centers. Cross held off on declaring a state of emergency, but Colonel Mapes, the director of Civil Defense operations warned Maine residents to stay far away from the shore. Storm tides were expected to hit the state by five or six o'clock in the evening, arriving without preceding high winds to warn locals.

Mapes' warning was one that many residents had already taken to heart. With the exception of a few police, soldiers, Civil Defense volunteers, and particularly stubborn residents, coastal cities and towns throughout the state were virtually abandoned, with people heading inland to stay with relatives. In expectation of storm tides, Popham Beach was cleared with the exception of one man with a mulish desire to stick out the storm on the beach.

By noon, Fred Ruoff, an American Red Cross organizer from Alexandria, Virginia, stationed in Waterville, Maine was proud to announce that all of the Red Cross chapters on the coast had set up their canteens and shelters. One of the trucks hauling generators back from Fort Devens experienced a snapped axle on the return journey, but otherwise, the day passed uneventfully as officials followed weather reports with bated breathe.

As the storm arrived, reports began to flood in just as floodwaters began to rise. York Hospital lost power and requested a backup generator, while water rose quickly, topping the Topsham-Brunswick bridge on the Androscoggin River by 4:30. A few daring motorists forged through the water on the bridge. Meanwhile, flooding closed Rte. 100 from Portland to Lewiston, Beach Street in Saco, Brighton Avenue in Portland, and Rte. 25 to Gorham. Lights flickered and died in Augusta and Eliot, with 5,000 phones disconnected in Eliot as well. In Richmond, flood waters raised several houses off their foundations. Two state police officers armed with 15 sticks of dynamite and blasting caps were dispatched to deal with the problem—presumably by blowing the errant homes up with the explosives. Civil Defense crews stocked with sandbags deployed to Dixmont High School where four foot flood waters were rapidly inundating the school. Although a few communities such as Bangor declared a state of emergency, the only serious worry in the state was for the Little River Dam in Belfast, which threatened to fail at any moment. The Maine National Guard quickly evacuated families living downstream of the dam.

During Hurricane Sandy, in 2012, many people complained about the news media's near hysterical efforts to 'hype' the storm. In fact, similar criticisms were leveled against the news in 1954.

E.B. White was living in Maine as Hurricane Edna approached the region. Although a writer by trade, and a very prominent one, White was well connected to the outside world with battery powered radios, and a bedside radio powered off a wall plug. White contributed some of his thoughts about the storm at the end of the month in the *New Yorker* magazine.

"Hurricanes are the latest discovery of radio stations and they are being taken up in a big way. To me, Nature is continuously absorbing -- that is, she is a twenty-four-hour proposition, fifty-two weeks of the year -- but to radio people, Nature is an oddity tinged with malevolence and worth of note only in her more violent moments." In White's belief, radio newscasters either ignored nature entirely, or gave natural hazards overwrought treatment, as with the arrival of Edna. He understood that the radio was needed to inform the public about dangerous, and potentially deadly storms. However, in White's view, "another effect of the radio is to work people up to an incredible state of alarm many hours in advance of the blow, while they are still fanned by the mildest zephyrs." Evidence for this came from one Civil Defense volunteer who died of a heart attack before Edna even arrived, in White's eyes, a victim of hurricane-induced anxiety.

White's diatribe about the radio's induced frenzy continued later on in the article. After eating breakfast, White and his entire family (with the exception of his pet dachsund) drifted to the radio. Broadcasts about the hurricane's ferocity reached every room in the house, "bringing ominous news."

White was puzzled by all of the "ominous" news. "As near as I could make out, the storm was still about a thousand miles away and moving north-northeast at about the speed of a medium-priced automobile." Several deaths had been reported in New Jersey, and fear in the storm's lead-up had resulted in state of emergency declarations in Connecticut and Portland, Maine. However, none of the locations had been struck yet.

White listened as the broadcasters spent time and energy attempting to keep the hurricane hysteria going. "During the morning hours, they were having a tough time keeping Edna going at the velocity demanded of emergency broadcasting." One radio reporter interviewed the station's man in the field, checking up on conditions in eastern Long Island from the safety of his car.

'How would you say the roads were?' asked the tense voice.

'They were wet,' replied the reporter, who seemed to be in a sulk.

'Would you say the spray from the puddles was dashing up around the mudguards?' inquired the desperate radioman.

"It was one of those confused moments, emotionally, when the listener could not quite be sure what position radio was taking -- for hurricanes or against them."

Coincident with the extensive blackouts during Carol and Edna, a consortium of New England companies announced that a new enterprise was being created. The Yankee Atomic Electric Company would seek approval from the Atomic Energy Commission to begin building pressurized water reactors to supply New Englanders with clean, "Atomic Age" electricity.

Arriving on the heels of Carol, Edna's impact was clear: lightning, or at least hurricanes, *could* strike twice.

Errant Edna

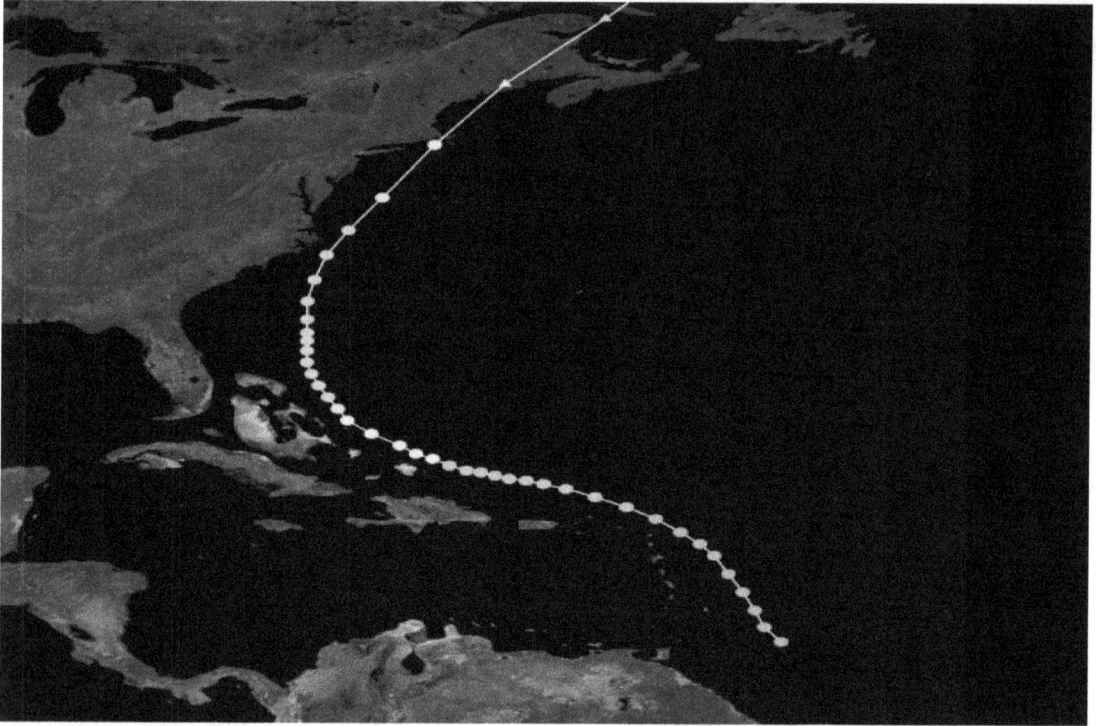

The path of Hurricane Carol from the Lesser Antilles to New Brunswick.

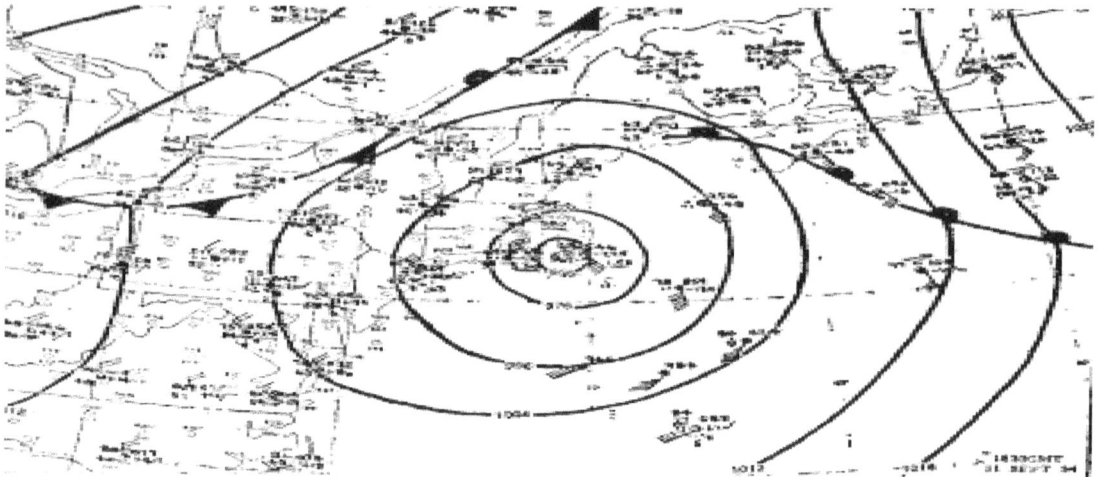

A surface weather map of Edna approaching New England.

Workers make temporary repairs along Maine's Rte. 24 following a washout.

A culvert washout on Rte 117 in Denmark, Maine, created by the storm, threatens to snarl passing vehicles. The dump truck may be hauling gravel for repair work.

Forecasting the Twisted Sisters

The 1950s were a time of growing awareness of the climate. Theories of potential global warming and complex computer climate models were still in the future, but radar was extending the range of forecasts, and allowing meteorologists to make more accurate predictions, even for events as unpredictable as hurricanes.

The Weather Bureau produced many of the national and regional forecasts during the 1950s. The present day National Weather Service (NWS) which succeeded the Weather Bureau, still shares many traits with its predecessor agency. Both agencies were organized within the federal Department of Commerce, although NWS was born from a 1970 Nixon-administration reorganization that created the National Oceanic and Atmospheric Administration (NOAA), the new parent agency for NWS. In addition to issuing weather forecasts on a daily basis and collecting climatic data, the NWS spots, tracks and issues alerts on every Atlantic tropical storm and hurricane.

Although predicting day-to-day weather was certainly a large part of the Weather Bureau's operations, tracking major storm systems was viewed as a high priority. In the Middle West, meteorologists kept a close watch on the flat plains for the first signs of tornadoes, whereas Atlantic field offices dealt with hurricanes, nor'easters, and other intense maritime storms. As a civilian agency, the Weather Bureau often cooperated with coastal military operations. With the Army-McCarthy hearings taking place in Washington as part of the national 'witch-hunt' for communists, and a nationwide sense of military significance, the Bureau was quick to remind legislators (and any readers interested enough to peruse their reports) about their close ties to the military. "In order to provide every possible warning to the public, a special hurricane forecasting unit operates at Miami, Florida, as a joint center with the U.S. Air Force and the U.S. Navy. [Information]....is obtained from vessels operating in the areas [suspected as storm 'breeding' grounds] and from Caribbean land stations. When occasions become suspicious, reconnaissance airplanes are sent to obtain more detailed information..." Although storm data was often gathered by civilian ships, the description of "vessels" made the Navy's involvement implicit.

Nevertheless, the military was a major source of meteorological data for the Weather Bureau. The services had trained and employed some of the most talented individuals in the weather field during World War II to issue forecasts in support of the war effort. Particularly in the 1950s, both the Air Force and Navy had access to the kind of high-tech equipment sought after by the Weather Bureau. Both services trained highly skilled pilots willing to brave the rough and uncertain conditions of a storm as 'Hurricane Hunters.' Similarly, both services were armed with a technology that was still in its infancy: radar.

Ships would gather humidity, air pressure and temperature information as they encountered the storm, or in the case of reconnaissance aircraft, as they penetrated the storm clouds. Whatever data resulted was processed and analyzed at the Miami joint center and wired by teletype to the Weather Bureau Office in New York City, as well as to other field offices elsewhere in the country. Miami would wire updates as a storm traveled up the coast, until the storm passed Cape Hatteras, at which point, the Washington National Airport field office would take charge of tracking and issuing alerts. Once the storm reached Block Island, off of southern Rhode Island, tracking and weather updates became the responsibility of the Bureau's Airport Station in Boston. At each step along the way, teletype updates would be sent to the New York office.

Forecasting put to use virtually every piece of 1950s mass communication. Alerts were sent between offices and relayed to news agencies using local teletype networks. Callers could seek information using "automatic telephone" networks. Weather updates would also travel by Coast Guard teletype, Western Union telegraph, and from ships via marine radio stations such as Mackay and RCA.

Two of the nation's biggest news agencies—NBC and CBS—opened up branches in the Bureau's 17 Battery Place office. The branches came complete with electrical engineers and broadcasters. Updates could be issued directly from the Bureau's office, by station broadcasters or government meteorologists. In other cases, smaller radio and TV stations relayed updates through direct telephone announcements. NBC and CBS were not alone. They shared the office with specialists from United Press and Associated Press, as well as from most major New York newspapers.

Unlike the 1938 and 1944 storms, which had been widely reported through radio stations and newspapers, the 1954 storms were among the first hurricanes reported on TV stations. Parts of the storms and their impact included scenes filmed on scene, "in the field," which were subsequently broadcast or edited into newsreels.

Forecast for Disaster: American Meteorology in the 1950s

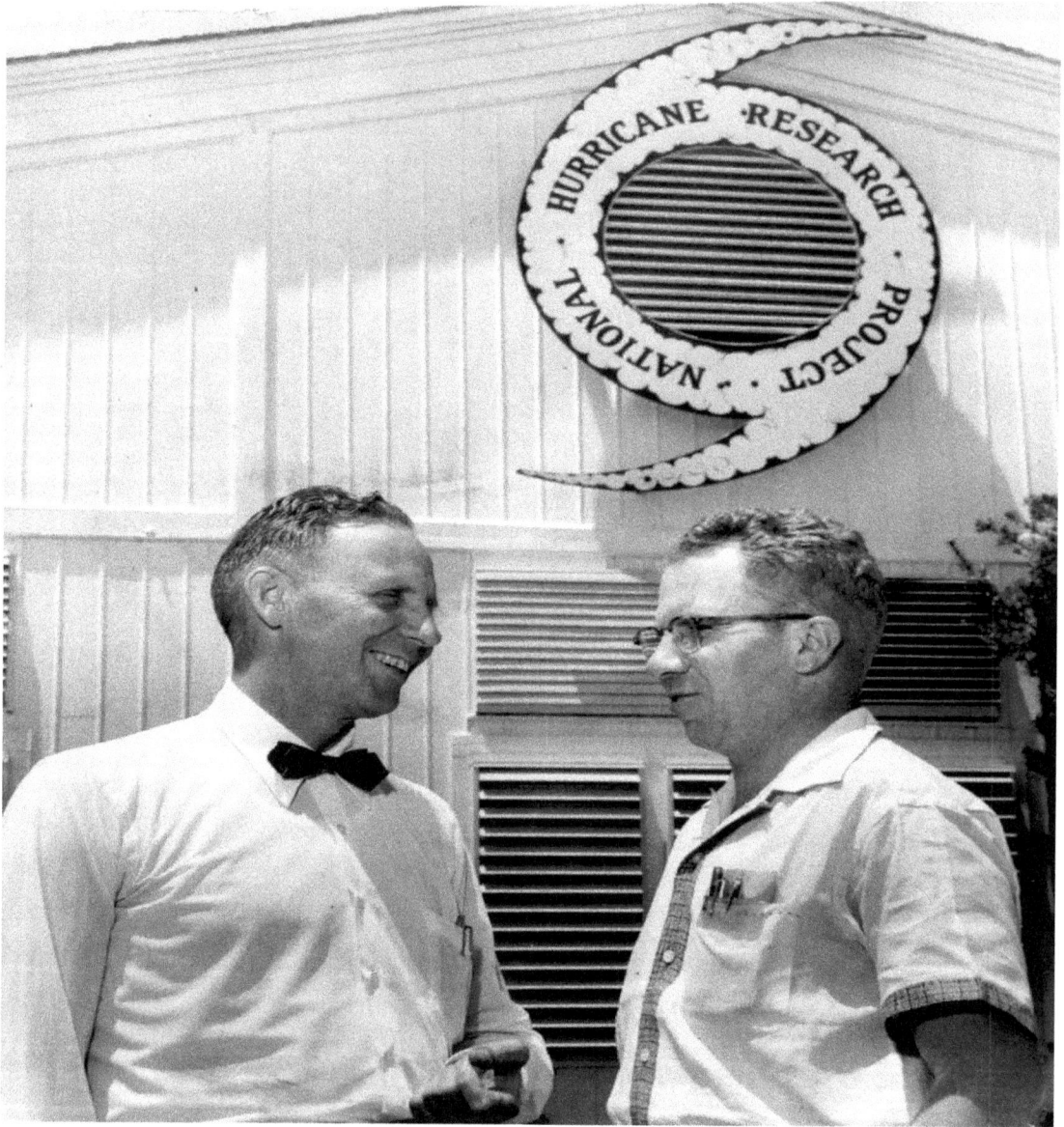

The National Hurricane Research Project was launched in 1955 by the Weather Bureau in Miami, Florida. This photo from April, 1956 shows Robert Simpson and Cecil Gentry sporting some very nice pocket protectors, a bowtie, and shirtsleeves to deal with a hot Florida spring.

The Lindsey Hopkins Building in Miami housed the Weather Bureau Office from 1948 until the late 1950s. Strangely, the WBO actually claimed a life—bureau chief Grady Norton died in 1954 after a 12 hour shift predicting Hurricane Hazel, due to a stroke. (Courtesy NOAA).

Although not the actual aircraft flown into Hurricane Edna by journalist Edward R. Murrow, the YB-29 (above) appears much the same as an aircraft that Air Force "Hurricane Hunters" flew into storms during the 1950s.

Journalist Edward R. Murrow (circa 1960).

Hurricane Connie—August 7-14, 1955—The Third Sister

Nearly a year had passed since the destruction caused by the Carol and Edna, and now it appeared that nature would mark the anniversary with another catastrophe. Some of the first news of Hurricane Connie reached New Englanders on August 7, 1955. The *Providence Journal* informed readers of a hurricane impacting the Caribbean, although there was little alarm initially. Surely, this one wouldn't head north too!

The outer edge of Hurricane Connie had skirted Puerto Rico and the US Virgin Islands. Although wind gusts had risen to 70 miles per hour, San Juan, the Puerto Rican capital, was the only location considered "badly" hit, as 50 mile per hour squalls struck the city. The eye of the storm actually passed 50 miles south of the position originally stated by the Weather Bureau. A "storm hunter" aircraft flew into the eye, confirming its actual location.

In San Juan, the storm led to power outages and flight cancellations, while in the nearby Virgin Islands, a Hollywood film crew, working on a World War II-themed picture, *The Proud and the Profane*, including actors Thelma Ritter, Deborah Kerr, and William Holden, was battered with high winds and rain. According to news reports, the northern portion of the storm was stronger than its southern edge. A weekend alert was issued for the southeastern US, but the storm remained 980 miles southeast of Florida, proceeding laterally at 15 miles per hour. It was far enough from the shore that the swirling, 125 mile per hour winds around the eye did not stand a chance of harming the coast, or anybody besides sailors.

Gordon Dunn, the chief Miami forecaster told the press, "It is still too early to forecast whether this hurricane will reach the mainland of the United States...We just don't want anyone to get out of touch and perhaps find a dangerous storm upon them without a warning." The storm was assigned a "C" name because it was the third storm of the season, and therefore, the third letter of the alphabet was selected for its name.

Back in New England, the hurricane was little more than an incidental story. In the Ocean State, the University of Rhode Island was proudly premiering its first part-time degree program in Providence. Adults of any age could pursue a bachelor of science, but unlike more "streamlined" 21st century programs, it would take five years of evening classes, and a sixth year of day classes to complete. The other leading story was that of a downed American airmen, recently released by the Chinese Communists, who told of, "persuasion that civilized people do not know about," used to coerce him into an espionage confession.

In Connecticut, a blistering heat wave left the state sweltering. Average daytime temperatures were as high as 91 degrees Fahrenheit, soaring to record-breaking highs of 102 degrees on some days. Bristol and Hartford County dairy farmers lost 90 percent of their second hay crop—needed to feed herds—as a result of the heat. Forecasters warned that the low 90s temperatures were, "only a breather." The *Hartford Courant* added its own "two-cents" worth. "Temperatures in the high 90s and 100-plus have frayed nerves, parched crops and put communities on short water rations from the Rockies eastward for more than a month."

By August 9th, Connie had approached to within 450 miles of the Florida coastline. The Weather Bureau issued a midnight advisory. Navy ships, weighed anchor, and left the confined waters of Hampton Roads, Virginia, while Marines at Cherry Point, North Carolina flew aircraft inland. Six volunteers at the Wilmington weather station stood by to issue telephone warnings to the surrounding area, while the Red Cross made preparations in Washington. Small craft warnings were put in place as, far north as Block Island.

August was the height of the polio season in New England, a season that may have worsened as a result of the hot weather. But families still flocked to the public places, such as pools, where the virus could spread much more easily. The two leading public health figures in Rhode Island held a radio press conference with the station WEAN. Dr. McAteer warned listeners that Jonas Salk's recently developed polio vaccine was only 60 percent effective against the worst forms of the disease. The day before the press conference, 775 children from 21 different Providence schools had received "second round" injections. Nevertheless, 46 people were confined to Charles V. Chapin Hospital, battling the often fatal illness.

As owners heeded government small craft warnings in Long Island Sound, and as the storm drew nearer, South County residents grew increasingly anxious. "Westerly, badly clobbered by three hurricanes in recent memory, got another case of the late summer jitters yesterday...Closing all beaches [because]of the heavy surf and strong undertow did not help the state of mind of the more timid." Hundreds of visitors, arriving after long drives, were disappointed to discover that Misquamicut beach was closed as a result of the heavy surf. In fact, heavy surf tore up part of Charlestown Beach Road, leaving five or six fishermen stranded along with their cars. Workers eventually filled in the gaps in the road, allowing them to drive off.

Life guards did not have great difficulty keeping people out of the water. Many families stayed home, listening to weather reports on their radio sets. WEAN and WPJB-FM were broadcasting hourly updates. In Galilee, the Atlantic Tuna Tournament had been moved up two weeks to avoid a repeat of the past year's disaster with Hurricane Carol. Now, the avid fishermen were, "mindful of what last year's hurricane did to the fleet..." The hulls reduced to matchwood made many reconsider the tournament. "We are all watching the weather very closely," tournament leader Walter McDonough told the press. Some vacationers in the towns of Narragansett and North Kingstown actually evacuated rather than face any danger from the storm.

The naval air stations at Quonset Point, Rhode Island and South Weymouth, Massachusetts, withdrew their planes to inland bases as far away as Kansas City. Off the coast of Cape Cod, a crew of 70 tradesmen continued work on a new "Texas Tower." Managed by the Air Force, the project called for creating a series of manned radar stations, rising from the waters of the continental shelf. Each tower would be equipped with radar to scan the Atlantic horizon for approaching Soviet bombers arriving from Europe, to warn shore based defenses. The Texas Tower in question was nearly complete—two of its 200 foot long steel legs had already been "sunk" into the seafloor, but a third needed to be put into place before the storm. Woods Hole Oceanographic

Institute predicted waves as high as 40 feet, which could easily swamp the tower's decking, which still lacked a helicopter pad, and almost any kind of shelter from the storm.

In Connecticut, New England Light and Power Co. crews were put on alert to respond to downed wires, while Governor Abraham Ribicoff prepared to fly back from a governor's conference in Chicago. The Blackstone Valley squadron of Civil Air Patrol volunteers readied to survey storm damage, setting up an emergency headquarters in one officer's Central Falls, Rhode Island home to communicate with three members' cars by short-wave.

Eastern Rhode Island braced for the storm as well, particularly the towns of Warren, Barrington and Bristol. Barrington lacked radios for its emergency crews and decided to rely on air raid sirens to warn the public. The sirens, mounted on top of the Berkshire-Hathaway mill (a regional manufacturing firm later made famous when it was bought by Warren Buffett and transformed into a multi-billion dollar holding company) would sound the alarm eight hours before the storm arrived. Bristol's sewage plant dismantled its pumps, bringing them to drier, higher ground, along with machine guns in the National Guard arsenal, which were taken to Warren. One Providence business painted a hurricane map on their boarded up, sandbagged store front to show passersby the path of the storm.

In spite of such widespread anxiety, the Weather Bureau's stance was much more relaxed. "...the Weather Bureau said [the storm's] loss of forward motion made it difficult to say when, or how close, it would come to New England," one Providence journalist wrote, adding for the sake of overconfident readers, "Meanwhile, Connie remained a formidable and dangerous storm with its winds continuing up to 135 miles an hour." The storm was in a "state of flux," essentially stalled off North Carolina because it had not encountered any upper air currents to steer it in a particular direction. The Weather Bureau had not upgraded its "alert" to a "warning," suggesting that the storm was less dangerous than the press and local governments seemed to think.

On August 12, the toss up on destructiveness was met with an answer. Power lines were downed and some houses were destroyed in North Carolina. At sea, off of New England, the terrifying waves prophesied by the Woods Hole did not materialize, although waves as high as 20 feet still battered the Texas Tower. Sixty men stayed onboard, while 43 were evacuated onboard a Navy tugboat. Although truly massive waves did not appear, heavy seas still complicated their return. Twenty-one of the evacuees were thrown into the raging waters, but thanks to kapok life-preservers, each one of them was rescued alive. A significant, but small news item also appeared in regional newspapers. A new hurricane had been born in the Caribbean, 470 miles northwest of Puerto Rico. It was dubbed Diane.

A day later, Connie finally struck the Northeast and Mid-Atlantic—with a somewhat mixed impact. Near its center, winds continued to circulate at a high rate of 115 miles per hour, although the storms horizontal movement averaged less than seven miles per hour. In Chesapeake Bay, 10 people drowned when their schooner broke up. Four were killed in Washington in a car accident caused in part by the storm, while New York

City witnessed six fatal casualties. The "Big Apple" experienced appalling rainfall—half a foot of rain reportedly fell in 24 hours.

August 14th, 1955 was the 10th anniversary of the Japanese surrender, an event celebrated in Rhode Island's VJ—Victory over Japan—Day. Hundreds of World War II veterans gathered at McCoy Stadium in Pawtucket to mark the event. The night before, "Hurricane Connie became a memory...for most Rhode Islanders."

The storm that had caused so much anxiety in the Ocean State, "blew itself out" over central Pennsylvania, leading to a drop in wind speed. The Weather Bureau in Boston reverted to small craft warnings around Block Island, signaling that danger had nearly disappeared. In Rhode Island, an average of 3.01 inches of rain fell, coupled with 46 mile per hour winds. Most of Massachusetts received an inch of rain, although Cape Cod—like New York City--received a high of 6.91 inches. The storm even proved to be somewhat of an entertainment event for Rhode Island residents. "Thousands of residents yesterday afternoon visited shore areas throughout the state, anticipating a thrill in witnessing nature in a violent mood. They were rewarded by the sight of heavy rolling seas and abnormal waves. But the tide level remained near normal, offering no threat to person or property."

The hurricane diminished into simply a larger storm on August 14th, as it passed over Lake Erie, although it continued to drop large quantities of rain along its route. New York state experienced an average total rainfall of 2.19 inches of rain, with a modest 1.11 inches falling at the state capital in Albany, and an astonishing 12.55 inches—more than foot—in New York City. Cleveland and Pittsburgh recorded 1.76 and 1.47 inches respectively, which mirrored similar readings of 1.82 inches in Burlington, Vermont. Showers associated with the hurricane moistened roads and farm fields throughout the eastern US, and extended as far west as Colorado and the Dakotas. At the Hillsgrove weather station in Rhode Island, Connie's passing gave staff members a brief respite and something to celebrate. Meteorologist Ralph Carlson had worked for 15 hours straight through the storm. The station's teletype had clattered steadily the whole time, sending updates to 17 private clients and 33 state police outposts. The station had recently purchased a facsimile (fax) machine that would speed up storm messages by as much as 90 minutes. However, the machine had yet to be hooked up. Although Connie proved to be somewhat of a non-event for Rhode Islanders, it added to public sentiment from the previous year—and the 1938 and 1944 storms—for an engineering solution to protect property and lives. An editorial in the *Providence Journal* encouraged private citizens to take measures of their own. "The threat posed to downtown Providence by Hurricane Connie disclosed that many building owners and businessmen still depend on makeshift emergency construction for protection against wind and water...No doubt it costs more to get pre-fabricated protective devices than it does to throw together a mass of sandbags and a barricade of raw wood for a single storm. But if we must live annually with hurricane threat, a long term investment in pre-cut devices may prove cheaper than jerry-built devices which must be newly created every time a hurricane alert is issued." The writer added a thought for the future. "Of course, the correct long-term answer to the problem of protection from water damage is the construction of barriers in the bay. But bay dams won't protect the plate glass from high winds and property owners ought to keep that in

—

mind if they're postponing the job of building their own protective devices because dams are to be built in time."

Unbeknownst to Americans living throughout the Northeast, the relatively mild Hurricane Connie was just a sampler of a much more dangerous storm charging up the coast, virtually on 'its heels.' Significantly, Connie produced heavy rainfalls that raised the water levels across the region from the tiniest streams to the largest rivers and lakes. Rains simultaneously waterlogged soils, preventing the further absorption of water in some locations.

Cunning Connie

Hurricane Connie Rainfall - August 11-14, 1955

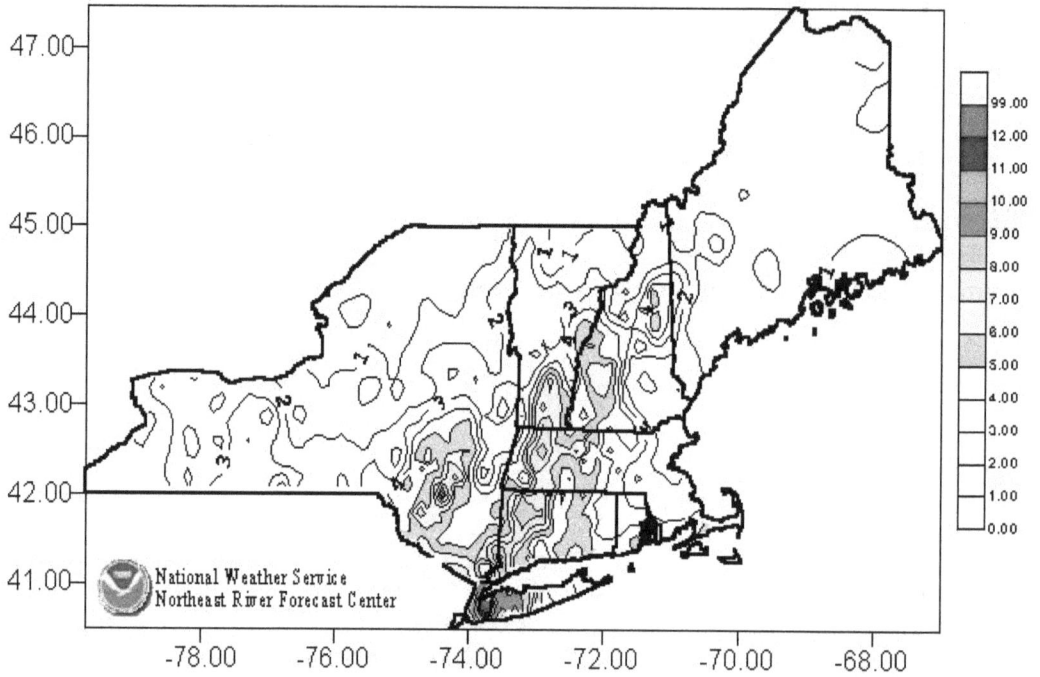

Connie's rainfall totals were tremendous, particularly in New York City and Long Island (see above). Forecasters snapped photos of Connie's appearance on the radar (below).

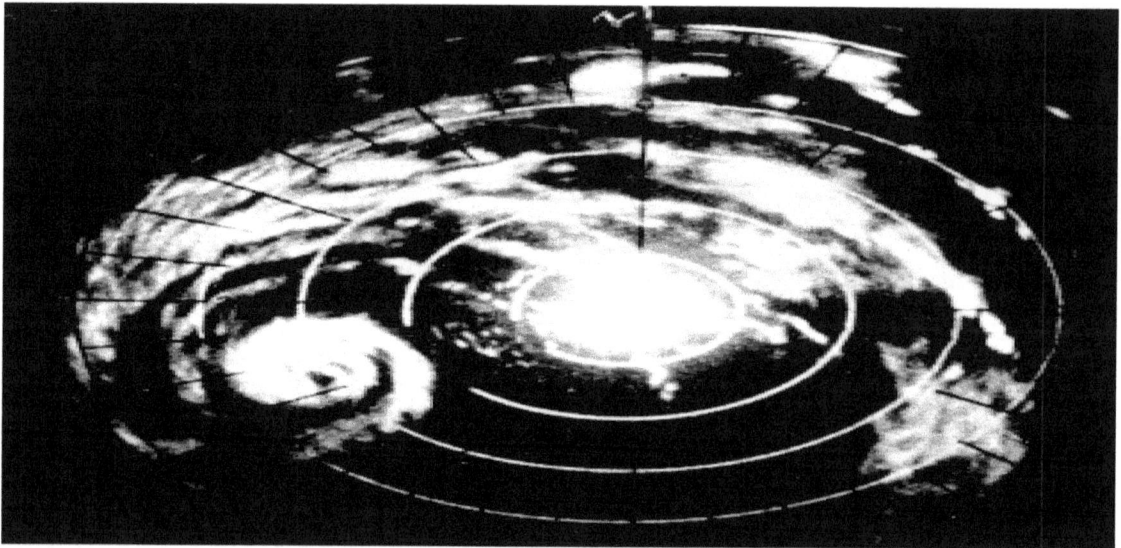

Hurricane Diane—August 11-17, 1955—The Fourth Sister

At seven in the morning, on August 11, 1955, the Miami field office issued an Advisory Number 1 for Tropical Storm Diane, forming from a tropical storm 400 miles to the northeast of San Juan, the Puerto Rican capital. The storm reports arrived from ships operating in the Caribbean. The Bureau's first bulletin announced that the storm was moving northwest at a speed of 14 miles per hour. Diane started off strong. Within the cyclone's center, winds reached between 50 and 60 miles per hour, while in the storm's 'tails' gale force winds greater than 100 miles per hour were observed. The Bureau sent aircraft to get a fix on the storm during the early afternoon and predicted that the storm would soon intensify.

By 11 a.m. the same morning, "meager reports" had placed the storm close to its original position, about 420 miles from San Juan. As military aircrews, aboard four-engine Lockheed Constellation patrol planes, known as "Willy Victors" by their navy crews, from their original WV-1 designation, flew out in search of Diane, they helped to set straight the ship reports. The Hurricane Hunters discovered that the storm was in fact 60 miles further north than the 11 a.m. bulletin had stated. Ships in the storm's path were urged to 'batten down the hatches' or leave the area, with the tropical storm expected to become a hurricane within 12 to 24 hours. Already, gale force winds were spread out across the ocean for 100 miles to the southeast and 200 miles to the northeast.

The storm soon impacted Myrtle Beach, South Carolina, and Cape Fear, raking both shores with 90 mile per hour winds. It was alarming news considering that Connie had left a body count of 43 in the Carolinas a few days earlier.

In New England, the casualty count began to grow before the bulk of the storm had even arrived.. Forty year old motorist, David Cutter, his wife Elsie, and three year old daughter, Patricia, were killed in Bolton, Vermont when rain-weakened earth gave way, burying his car in a landslide along Rte. 2. Frederick Kinnicutt, a Navy yeoman serving in Newport, drowned in undertow at Second Beach in Middletown, Rhode Island. Three of his shipmates plunged into the water to try to save his life, but nearly drowned themselves. Elsewhere in southern Rhode Island, a 45-year old woman drowned when her skiff capsized at Point Judith.

Compared with the slow response to Carol and Edna a year earlier, the Weather Bureau believed that it was well situated to deal with the latest storm. One meteorologist told the press, "We've come a long way with hurricanes in the past year, but there are so many more things that can still be accomplished." In fact, the dissemination of information about the1955 storms was much better than 1954. The Weather Bureau had worked hard to sooth the public about Connie, while also providing valuable information about where it might strike, and with what intensity. After the Hurricane Carol debacle, New England legislators were encouraged to support the Weather Bureau so that a mistake of that magnitude would not happen again. "In its unusually successful campaign for more money from Congress, the Weather Bureau and its New England congressional allies laid out a comprehensive program for immediate and long-range improvements in research, observations, and coordination and transmission of warnings, forecasts, and hurricane news," one *Providence Journal* writer noted.

More than wind, it was rain that defined Diane. By the time the storm reached New England, it was described as, "dying" by the press. In many respects, Diane was a dying storm, with its dropping wind velocities. But for a storm just clinging, it certainly had quite a bit of life left in its clouds. Rainfall in western Massachusetts washed out the soil beneath the railroad tracks in Russell, sending two engines and three cars of the Chicago-Boston liner off the tracks. A baggage car plunged into the Westfield River, while one of the coaches dangled "crazily" on the tracks. Forty-four year old Stanley Knott, from Natick, Massachusetts, was in the baggage car when it when it went 'into the drink.' He smashed through a window and swam to safety. Fortunately, only 30 people suffered minor injuries because the train had only been traveling at 18 miles per hour at the time of the derailment, preventing a far worse accident.

The line in Russell was not the only one disrupted by the storm. Trains throughout eastern Massachusetts were cancelled or ran late. A similar washout of the New Haven railroad in Sharon, Massachusetts closed the track and busses were brought in to ferry passengers between Providence and Boston. Most eastbound trains from Rhode Island were rerouted through Walpole, and passengers from Rhode Island got off at the Rte. 128 stop, as a result of eight inches of water on the tracks at Back Bay and South Station, leading to a 50 minute delay. Motorists were also impacted. Four people, including a

Providence youth, were critically injured during a three-car collision in Seekonk. Rte. 1 in Dedham and numerous other highways in eastern Massachusetts and Rhode Island flooded, leaving motorists stalled on the inundated roads.

Although wind and rain did whip coastal areas, Diane's impact was felt almost immediately in northern Rhode Island. Power outages were fairly modest, with 20 families in Cumberland losing electricity, but water was somewhat more concerning. "A belting rain, backlash of dying Hurricane Diane struck Rhode Island yesterday with the Blackstone Valley area the hardest hit." Between midnight and 9:30 a.m. Woonsocket measured 4.45 inches of rain, a rate that if stretched over 24 hours would amount to nearly a foot. "The city appeared most affected by the storm with roads left with gullies and washouts," the *Providence Journal* reported.

The following day, Woonsocket was seeing the effects of all the rain that had fallen. Correspondent James Marshall stepped into a telephone booth, slipped in a handful of coins and asked the operator to connect him to the *Providence Journal.* "I am standing in a telephone booth on Social Street in Woonsocket about 500 yards from Social and Cumberland Street. Looking out of the booth I can see the water, which is approximately four feet deep at the intersection. I can see the water smashing windows of stores along the two streets. The water, which is flowing like small rapids along Cumberland Street, as a result of the break at the Horseshoe Falls at the Massachusetts border, is forcing families in the Social Street area to evacuate."

Chief of police, Edgar Turcotte, ordered a street-by-street evacuation of families, particularly along Brook Street. One family refused to leave their apartment with auxiliary police even though four feet of water in the street threatened to undermine their foundation. Marshall continued, "The water is rising at better than a foot a minute. At the rate it is now rising, the outdoor phone booth in which I am standing will be flooded in 10 or 15 minutes... Large chunks of debris that were probably part of the display windows in stores in this area can be seen bobbing crazily along Cumberland Street...Police and rescue workers find themselves helpless in the face of this threat of nature, but sit and watch the rising waters." On Social Street, the water was flowing as fast as 15 miles per hour. In fact, the current was so strong along North East Street that four state lifeguards were called in. They used rescue reels and buoys to help people across, including an elderly disabled woman, as well as a man named Odilion Jacques, his wife, and nine children.

Further down the Blackstone River valley other regional cities faced similar challenges. "Pawtucket was a city on the alert last night as city officials and residents keep vigil along the banks of the Blackstone River, which was rising at 11:30 p.m. at the rate of four inches an hour." Pawtucket mayor, Lawrence McCarthy, closed Main Street in the early evening. As darkness fell, hundreds of spectators watched the river's level rise. At the Collyer Insulated Wire Company, water was creeping up behind the factory. A flashlight inspection revealed that the water levels were approaching the same level as the 1936 flood.

Over the course of the night, conditions worsened in both Pawtucket and Woonsocket. The lower floors of several Pawtucket factories were flooded. Damaged companies included the Collyer factory, Paramount Printing and Finishing, and Vesta Underwear. Twenty feet of water filled the basement of City Hall. Several inches trickled into the basement of the historic Slater's Mill—the birthplace of the Industrial Revolution in America. A pre-existing retaining wall was the only thing that spared City Hall and Slater's Mill from being washed away. The city's bridges were a major area of concern. The Main and Exchange Street bridges were both closed to traffic, snarling the downtown with cars. Out of 50 Civil Defense volunteers in the city, a handful spotted a group of children watching the rising waters by the old Blackstone Avenue footbridge, and shooed them away. It proved fortuitous when, not long after, the tons of debris piling up against the bridge caused it to give way.

Rumors circulated that the Main Street bridge and its neighboring retaining wall were about to wash away. "Both were subjects of constant concern by city officials as logs, huge trees, and parts of buildings battered the bridge and as splits and leaks developed in the WPA [Work Projects Administration]-built retaining wall which refused to bow to the might of what old timers called the worst flood ever seen in Pawtucket." Water sloshed dangerously over the retaining wall, leading one city official to comment, "It's liable to go any second now." Along Roosevelt Avenue storefronts were destroyed, and basements waterlogged. Even with water drowning the city, Pawtucket residents could not seem to quench their own thirst. The Embassy Bar stayed open until the evening, serving bottled beer and tapping into its kegs, until it was shut down by a health inspector.

—

Not far to the north, along the river, Woonsocket remained a closed-city by order of Chief Turcotte, who shut the roads to private vehicles. Six National Guard companies and 350 state Department of Public Works employees patrolled the streets, cleaning up debris. Surprisingly, 90 percent of city customers still had working telephones, but on a very local, neighborhood level, flood damage was severe. No fatalities had been reported, but many people were newly homeless. "Horror and despair gave ground slowly yesterday in Woonsocket's flood-torn northern district. Hard-working cleanup crews piled silt, drifted lumber, ruined furniture and long swaths of spoiled cloth from textile mills into state and city trucks...Residents of the flooded tenement area, who has spent the night in emergency shelters or with relatives, returned during the day to inspect their caved-in dwellings and mired cars." Reporter John Skow tagged along with councilman Edward Shaw and building inspector Albert Lapierre for a tour of the city. "A family of four sat quietly on the first floor porch of a tenement whose foundation was missing for most of its front length. 'We'll be all right,' said the husband, a rugged looking man in work clothes. He pointed to a 2-by-4 [board] he had wedged under the unsupported corner of the building. A patrolman disagreed and told them they would have to move by 4 p.m."

The group encountered one man on East Street who was trying to move his car out of the water. "It floated a quarter mile last night," he told them. The entire neighborhood was stirred up when two dump trucks passed carrying bodies from Precious Blood Cemetery. Over 200 bodies were disinterred from the cemetery during the flood, but only five had been recovered at the time of Skow's visit. The Civil Defense Administration issued metal containers for any bodies that were recovered, and assigned undertakers from

James Heffernan's funeral home in Pawtucket to segregate recent drowning victims from the long-dead.

At the pioneer Ann&Hope discount store in Cumberland, east of Woonsocket, employees set up what looked like a giant rummage sale in the lot. In fact, it was merchandise piled outside to dry. The flood did not dampen everyone's spirits. Burrillville, a town situated to the west of Woonsocket in the state's northwestern corner experienced its worst flooding since 1938. At the village of Pascoag, the Hope family was distracted with preparations for a wedding and did not notice the water flooding their yard, at least at first. When the Hopes realized what was happening, they packed the children off to stay with family in nearby Harrisville. However, in spite of the flood, Evelyn Rita Hope married anyway, right on schedule.

Woonsocket's closest neighboring community, Blackstone, Massachusetts, was also impacted by river flooding. "Deluged by the swirling waters were the Blackstone Town Hall, including the second District Court building, and Roosevelt Park where the grandstand and bleachers were ripped apart." Four feet of water covered Main Street, and 20 feet in the high school gymnasium left it anything but dry. Ten businesses in the Monument Square section of town were also flooded.

The days after Diane helped to give Rhode Islanders an understanding of the challenges ahead. Woonsocket may have been the hardest hit community in the Blackstone River valley. One hundred sixty-six families were homeless, and 40 buildings were condemned. "Gaping holes representing condemned and razed buildings may mark

—
88

the destructive path taken by the Mill River as that normally placid little stream raged uncontrolled through Woonsocket's Social District." The discrepancy between the homeless and the number of buildings was due in large part to the large number of tenant families, living in ubiquitous 'triple-decker' apartment buildings who lost their housing with the storm.

Many of the region's mills and factories were located along the river, and its tributaries, because of historic reliance on waterpower for production. As a result, many industries had been 'flooded out,' idling 6,000 workers indefinitely. In fact, half of Woonsocket's workforce was idled, leading one journalist to comment, "Unquestionably the havoc wreaked by the flood has dealt a major blow to Woonsocket's widely-heralded efforts to revive the city's flagging economy." Two dozen mills in the valley were inundated, some covered by as much as 20 feet water. Murky pools surrounding the Alice Mill, home of the US Rubber Company, Woonsocket's largest employer, foretold a six week period before it would reopen. On Singleton Street, Jacob Finkelstein and Sons idled 500, while the Manville Mill in Lincoln (immediately south of Woonsocket) was virtually destroyed. Its expensive machinery and 400 employees became economic casualties. Further down the valley, toward Pawtucket, damage was less severe, but many mills were not predicted to reopen for several weeks.

The Bay State was targeted, too. As Diane approached New York City from the south at a speed of 15 miles per hour, the Boston Weather Bureau predicted "occasional thunderstorms." However, what they did not predict was, "A devastating torrential rainstorm..." in Central Massachusetts.

The *Worcester Telegram*, the largest newspaper in Central Massachusetts reported on the rising waters in the city and neighboring communities with increasing alarm on August 19th. "Torrential day long rains punished already waterlogged Worcester Thursday...The rains due to warm, moist air pushed north by Hurricane Diane, caused heavy damage in most of Central Massachusetts." Worcester received 4.93 inches of rain by 10 p.m., a rainfall record exceeded only two other times between 1903 and 1955. Southeast of the city, in Charlton, 18 people were evacuated from their homes, after police spotted water as deep as five feet in parts of Rte. 20. The Aldrich Manufacturing Company's dam overflowed near the State Police barracks. An additional eight people were evacuated from their homes by the Charlton City Post Office, which was filling with water. Local officials sandbagged the post office, in hopes of saving it from further flooding.

Months later, the Charlton selectmen in the town's annual report would describe August 19, 1955 as, "The most tragic day in the history of the Town of Charlton."

They continued, "Brooks, rivers, ponds and lakes filled to capacity from the rains of a hurricane called Diane, overflowed their banks and became monsters of destruction. Dams washed away turning millions of gallons of water loose upon our community and upon others as well." Unfortunately, the waters did not simply disappear into a swamp, a lake or an impound. Instead, "Homes, highways, bridges and [other] essential facilities were swept away by the raging waters."

Severe damage at the Charlton Woolen Company as a result of the flooding was a modest tragedy compared with the loss of five lives in the community. The rains knocked down the Carpenter Mill Dam and the Glen Echo Lake Dam, compounding the disaster.

Downstream, it was even worse.

Much of Greater Worcester felt the storm. Early in the day, traffic on the roads in Sturbridge, Charlton, and Brimfield nearly came to a halt, and westbound tractor-trailers had to be rerouted through Southbridge. Factories in Warren closed at mid-afternoon, after churning brooks washed out part of a new toll road—the Massachusetts Turnpike, then under construction, and a small bridge. Warren's town wells came under threat when water levels spiked in Comins Pond. Meanwhile, in Millbury, water levels were spiking in the Blackstone River. The river rose two feet in only two hours. Small scale washouts and flooding impacted West Millbury and Leicester. Sections of Stowe Road and Brightside Street in Buck's Village flooded enough to stop traffic, and in parts of Leicester, children paddled row boats around flooded yards.

The only recent reference point for the sheer volume of rain that fell, was in fact, the 1954 storms. Carol and Edna each exceeded the rainfall totals for a single day set by Diane. Carol dropped 5.07 inches and Edna dropped even more—6.16 inches; more than half a foot. August, 1955 witnessed a rainfall total of 8.96, even higher than the previous record for August, 1954 of 8.74 inches. Prior to 1954, the highest recorded totals had

———

occurred in 1927, which was also a year of regional flooding. Curiously, Diane was initially less destructive than Carol or Edna, both of which were accompanied by high winds.

Frederick Guerin, an engineer for the state DPW said of the rain, "We've taken quite a deluge." The deluge claimed nearly eight million dollars damage to a state highway project. In front of the Court House on Main Street, an under construction vehicular tunnel filled with water.

Few Massachusetts communities could claim damage on par with Southbridge. Flooding in the small manufacturing city, located along the Quinebaug River, southwest of Worcester, was reported as far away as Germany: "Flutkatastrophe in Nordamerika...in Southbridge im Staate Massachusetts."

The, "lashing offshoot of Hurricane 'Diane' sent the Town of Southbridge into an emergency evacuation operation...sending Civil Defense, Fire and Police officials into immediate action in rescue of persons living in extremely flooded areas," reported the *Southbridge Evening News.* Within a matter of hours, over one million dollars of damage took place in town, as the West Street dam burst and the Central Street bridge collapsed. By 10 a.m. the emergency evacuation was already under way, under orders from police chief, Ovide Desrossiers.

Throughout the neighboring communities of Dudley, Oxford, and Sturbridge, as well as Southbridge itself, winds tore down electrical and phone lines and choked streets with water. Every business closed and residents joined forces to put together supplies for evacuees, living in temporary quarters set up by Civil Defense. At 6:25 in the morning, Southbridge and its Quinebaug valley neighbors were shut off from the outside world, when every major road and highway was flooded. Rte. 20 in Sturbridge had already been blocked for 11 hours after, "onrushing torrents of flood waters," released by the shattered dam, struck the roadway and the Sturbridge Yankee Workshop. The waters arrived so rapidly that they stripped telephone poles, ruined the workshop's foundation, and even toppled steel fire hydrants, adding more water to the flow.

The water excavated large holes in all of the main roads leading through Oxford, while Dudley experienced dam breaks of its own. Considering the suddenness of the disaster, Southbridge responded quickly. Red Cross volunteers set up an emergency shelter at the Town Hall to handle an influx of frightened families, including large numbers of children who would need to be fed and housed. Collaborating with the Red Cross, were a variety of businesses and fraternal organizations, including the Redmen, Elks, Eagles, VFW, Knights of Columbus, the Congregational, Baptist and Notre Dame churches, as well as Like-Nu Cleaners, who opened their buildings to house disaster victims.

As perhaps the largest town in the Quinebaug River valley, Southbridge became an epicenter for the severe flooding that impacted the area. Harrington Hospital—the region's main hospital—put out an emergency call for milk and cream for formula-fed babies. Like the North Coventry, Connecticut milkman the year before, delivery drivers answered the call, gunning the engines of their milk trucks and driving into the submerged streets, hoping that their engines would not flood.

The *Southbridge Evening News* described the scene of chaos, "Heartbreak and misery walked hand in hand today...Much of the flood damage was in the Flats section of town where water ran down Central Street on to Charlton, Worcester and Mechanic Street...Eippe's super market was protected with sandbags. Cellars of stores and businesses in that section were filled to the ceiling. During evacuation early this morning, police carried women and children across the streets. Cars stranded on Mechanic Street had to be pushed by town highway department trucks." The dam breaks in Charlton, particularly the break at the Glen Echo Lake Dam, sent a vast discharge of water racing down Quinebaug's Cady Brook tributary and the Quinebaug River itself. In Southbridge, storm waters knocked down the West Street Dam, flooding the Globe Village section of the town. "Cement buildings were split and shattered and debris was piled against company ground fences."

Getting out the word about evacuations became a primary goal. New England Telephone &Telegraph employee, Edward Sullivan, indicated that lines between Southbridge and Worcester were down. Instead, emergency telephone lines through Webster would help officials to coordinate the relief effort. Southbridge in the 1950s was a city of villages. Although densely populated, and closely situated together, each neighborhood had its own unique geography. Southbridge Center slopes downhill but occupies generally high ground. By contrast, Globe Village and the Flats occupy low-lying ground around the Quinebaug. When the West Street dam gave out, shortly before 11 a.m. it swept away three houses in Globe Village, and the Central Street Bridge at 11:10. The police soon put out the call for rowboats and outboard engines to rescue people still stranded in Globe Village and the Flats. A bridge on Mashapaug Road also washed out, "marooning several dozen families," in the Westville part of town.

All told, 400 families were evacuated, and placed in emergency shelters at the police station, fire station, town hall, Notre Dame church, Knights of Columbus hall, and the local radio station, WESO. Additional space was provided by the school superintendent who opened up the schools to evacuees. Even on Main Street, a foot of water drenched the downtown, severing Rte. 131. In 1955, the Eisenhower Interstate System had yet to be created, and Rte. 20 was a main route between New York City and Boston. McLellan's and Edwards, neighboring local stores, both had flooded basements, although the damage may have been worse at Edwards, given the store's "bargain basement." After all, much of their merchandise was being stored in a perfect trap for floodwater.

To the east, Norfolk County communities weathered the storm much better than similar communities in Central Massachusetts. In Franklin and Medway, Massachusetts, two towns situated between the small cities of Milford and Attleboro, 12.68 inches of rain fell during Hurricane Diane, leading to a minor dam burst. The boundary between the two communities is defined in part by the Charles River, and Mine Brook in Franklin is a small tributary of the larger river. A small, old mill dam on Mine Brook near Beaver Pond helped to contain the waters of the man-made Mine Brook Pond, used to power a neighboring mill. During the storm, the small dam broke, draining the pond into the brook. The sudden torrent raced through western Franklin, along Grove Street, one of the town's main byways. The water knocked down a second small dam at Golding's mill pond, adding more water to the flood. The water left the bed of the brook, and swept the asphalt off of Grove Street, before disappearing into the swamps around the brook, on the other side of the road. The floodwaters reappeared in Medway, flooding low-lying parts of the downtown and covering Village Street in several feet of water.

A day after the torrential rains, water continued to rise throughout Massachusetts. In Auburn, near Worcester, 60 families—totaling more than 200 people--were moved to safety in the high school where a shelter was set up by the Red Cross. Like Southbridge, Sturbridge and Webster, Auburn was completely isolated for a period of time. At least three feet of water had poured into the town's Drury Square during the peak of the storm, flooding offices such as the Auburn News, Hall's Store, and the Post Office. To fulfill the Post Office creed, workers moved the office into the attic.

Governor Christian Herter made a public announcement to state residents. "All citizens [must] stay off the roads, especially in areas where repairs are being made and to undertake no trips whatever, unless definitely advised by the State Police...that the particular route of travel has been cleared." Herter added in his address, that the level of the Connecticut River would not be known until the following day. Shortly after speaking, the phone rang. Governor Lane Dwinnell from New Hampshire and Governor Edmund Muskie from Maine offered to help Massachusetts in any way possible.

With communications still spotty, Worcester radio stations such as WTAG pitched in to help. Norma Lesser was driving home through New Hampshire, returning from a vacation. She grew concerned about her parents' safety in Worcester and sent a telegram to the WTAG office from Keene. In the telegram, she asked the station to call her parents and broadcast any news of them. She would keep the dial locked to WTAG to hear the news. Clare Cassidy, a folk singer working for the station, telephoned Lesser's parents and then broadcast the bulletin, assuring her of their well being.

WTAG was not alone. All of Worcester's TV and radio stations pitched in to help. WAAB, WNEB, and WORC cleared their line-ups and switched to broadcasting emergency communications and messages on behalf of separated families. At WTAG, a litany of cancellations, warning messages, personal communications, and official instructions began arriving at six o'clock in the morning. Holding down one of the most important desks in the city, WTAG community service director, Andrew Fuller, managed an invisible switchboard of incoming and outgoing messages. All day and into the night, it was Fuller's job to decide what would air and when. Over the coming days, the *Telegram* dubbed him the "clearing house" for most of the emergency messages in the city. To keep people's spirits up throughout the crisis, WTAG kept some its regular programs running, but cut in frequently with new bulletins.

Jim Little, the news director for WTAG moved to Worcester's Civil Defense headquarters at 10 a.m. on Friday. Using a phone in the auditorium, Little patched through from Civil Defense headquarters to WTAG to broadcast right away. During the day, Little reported over the phone, soothing Worcester residents along with City Manager McGrath and Mayor O'Brien who took turns on the line.

WTAG broadcast jointly on AM and FM frequencies at different times of day. To extend the reach of their broadcasts, Little instructed the station to begin simultaneous FM broadcasts at 11 o'clock in the morning—five hours earlier than usual. Outsiders interested in passing along updates on the disaster phoned into WTAG. One of the station's newsmen, Dick Wright, broadcast over the telephone through WKNE, in Keene, New Hampshire and WBSM in New Bedford.

Friday afternoon, Little stepped away from his post in the auditorium and joined the station's mobile unit to drive around the city, with meteorologist Bill Ostberg. The team must have stopped frequently. Ostberg telephoned in at different points to broadcast updates, while Little recorded his own commentary and interviews with people along the way, which he broadcast in the evening, after returning to the auditorium.

Over at WAAB, Little's opposite number, George Downey stayed at the station, but kept it focused on the storm's aftermath with steady reports from staff members and the Associated Press. WAAB reporters visited each of the six "critically" flooded areas in the city. WWOR-TV kept viewers at home up to date, showing film and pictures of the flooding. Brown, one of the station's reporters, was stuck in Leicester, but continued to gather material for the station. WORC and WNEB did similar work, sending out bulletins, although WNEB's news director joined Jim Little at the auditorium, and managed to get Weather Bureau bulletins from Logan Airport on the air.

Many unusual stories emerged from the Worcester flood. A 13-year old boy may have been the city's youngest looter. He was arraigned in Juvenile Court after breaking into a house on Main Street on Friday, to steal a wallet containing $3.22. Other peculiar stories from the storm included the LaCasse family from Quebec. The husband and wife, vacationing with their three month old daughter, were stranded at a Red Cross shelter in the city, seeing a different side of Worcester's hospitality. With so many streets flooded, particularly in Webster Square, St. John's Cemetery became one of the busiest thoroughfares in the city as emergency vehicles were routed through narrow paths between rows of headstones.

Together with the out-of-sorts LaCasse family, over 100 people took shelter with the Red Cross in the Worcester Auditorium. Thirty minutes after City Manager McGrath declared a state of emergency, Civil Defense set up a communications hub in the auditorium, relaying messages between Civil Defense volunteers, police and fire workers. The phone rang off the hook, with over a thousand calls during the day. "Besides the calls reporting trouble, there were those volunteering help—either boats or a strong back." In fact, Civil Defense received offers of 30 different boats, with some owners calling from as far away as Fitchburg and Leominster. On top of its substantial urban emergency services, Worcester was able to muster at least 100 Civil Defense volunteers. The numbers were inexact, because many people stayed put in flooded areas, working with direction from city headquarters. In addition to hungry evacuees, the Red Cross dealt with first aid for people of all ages, including many visitors from out of town.

In parts of the city, lights—and generators—were beginning to fail. At least a few lights stayed on at the Worcester County Jail, allowing the sheriff's deputies to keep order. Lights flickered out at the Millbury Street School, which was in use as an emergency shelter. At the First National Store, a generator disappeared from view and electrified the surrounding water. As midnight approached, "frogmen" splashed through flooded areas to assess the damage. Although more calls for evacuations came in, and new washouts were discovered, the inspection brought good news. In places, the water was beginning to recede. At several factories, including the American Steel & Wire Division and Mountain Waterproof, small numbers of workers were stranded and boats were dispatched to bring them food and clean water.

Although the damage in Central Massachusetts and Rhode Island was tremendous, it pales in comparison to the much greater damage in Connecticut, for which Diane showed a special fury.

Waters rose swiftly throughout the state's rivers on August 19th and 20th quickly inundating roads, towns and cities. Drivers leaving Hartford ran into trouble on a temporary road below the Hartford-Springfield Expressway overpass, when water closed the road. Riders on the New Haven Railroad weren't much better off. Tracks flooded for 2,000 feet on the Winsted-Waterbury line. Elsewhere, in the Burrville section of

Torrington, another 1,000 feet flooded. Trains traveling in both directions stopped in Torrington. Passengers and mail traveled by bus to get to Winsted.

For people headed to Winsted, the town offered little better than the rain-choked roads and rails. Main Street and sections of Rte. 44 flooded in the community. Five inches of rain during the height of the storm were making themselves felt in Winsted. A block of concrete in a storm drain connecting the Gilbert Home Brook to the Mad River caved in, causing an eight foot flood in the basement of a neighboring school. Nevertheless, Winsted locals breathed a sigh of relief. A flood control project built in the aftermath of the Hurricane of '38 held back the Mad River throughout the storm. Torrington's Civil Defense director, Ann Lacey, commented on the difficulty of the recovery work in her town.

According to a letter, sent on December 2, 1955 by Leo J. Mulcahy, a local Civil Defense leader to A.D. O'Connor, the regional Civil Defense administrator in Newton, Massachusetts, volunteers in Winsted had received serious damage to their cars during rescue work. Winchester's Civil Defense director, Harold Drake ordered Edith Negri, Philip Sherman, and Frank Rockefellow to drive their cars into the town's "stricken areas" to rescue people. Rockefellow's car sustained $1,000 damage—almost its entire value. Mulcahy asked Civil Defense to reimburse the volunteers who had nearly sacrificed their vehicles in service to the community.

Torrington's Newfield Road Bridge and many of the town's main thoroughfares washed out, and heavy rains interrupted clean-up. Repair crews cleared storm drains of debris, just in time for them to fill up with more. In north central Connecticut, 80 families were evacuated from the Granbrook Park housing development in East Granby as Salmon Brook overflowed its banks. A similar situation forced the evacuation of 15 families (with 50 more prepared to flee) along the Farmington River.

Other communities saw water rising, but not to the same levels witnessed in Farmington, Granby, Torrington, and Winsted. Oil burners were disconnected in Windsor Locks and Barkhamsted as a foot of water accumulated in cellars. Capitol Avenue, Blue Hills Avenue, and Albany Avenue flooded in Hartford, although the water was highest in the Capital Avenue underpass, reaching the roofs of cars.

As time went on, things did not improve in Hartford. The Park River 'rampaged' overflowed its banks and flowing into nearby neighborhoods. Hundreds of families were evacuated from Rice Heights, Charter Oak Heights, Hawthorn Street and Hillside Avenue. Along Woodbine, Laurel, and Riverside Street, water was so high that DUKW amphibious vehicles, boats, and bosun's chairs strung on steel cables were needed to rescue people from their homes.

Initial reports from across the state indicated 38 people missing or dead—most of them children. Trestles and rail bridges were swept out by the flood waters along with roads and road-bridges. Homes toppled, foodstuffs and drinking water supplies were drenched with sewage and mud. Northwestern Connecticut, the Naugatuck river valley, and the area around Torrington and Winsted were the hardest hit locations in the state, but almost everywhere experienced some damage. Keeping with the level of damage in its namesake valley, Naugatuck's Memorial Bridge was swept away, cutting the town in two. Police and fire services evacuated to higher ground as their stations flooded.

At one in the morning, the Connecticut National Guard was mobilized. Governor Ribicoff ordered 16 helicopters into the Naugatuck River Valley and other hard hit locations. Soon after, the Navy contributed another 16 helicopters, together with eight from the Sikorsky plant in Stratford and two from the Kaman helicopter plant in Bloomfield.

Harry Neuman, a photographer with the Sikorsky Aircraft Division flew over the state aboard one of many rescue helicopters, and relayed his story to the *Hartford Courant* at the end of the day. "One man that we picked up clung hysterically at the pilot's leg and sobbed. Another man handed us his cat and refused to come aboard, he was so frightened." Neuman added, "We had to knock him out and drag him into the helicopter.'

"I've covered some bad Ohio floods for the Coast Guard but in all my life I never saw anything like this. We flew over Waterbury, Ansonia, and Naugatuck. We saw whole factories and trailer camps covered by water. We saw a theater and a school building collapse in Waterbury and in Naugatuck small rescue boats that were launched overturned in the swift current."

Sikorsky ultimately contributed 12 helicopters to the rescue effort. Not all of them were equipped with rescue gear. One pilot improvised a hoist from a rope and a tire to lift people off of roofs. "Most of the people we picked up, even the uninjured, were terribly frightened, of course. Some hesitated to get into the helicopters because of their markings.

One had Canadian insignia and the rescued woman thought she was being picked up by the Canadian Navy."

"'How could this happen?' one passenger cried. 'Nothing like this ever happened before.'"

"An elderly woman we rescued was almost unconscious. She had only a few soaking shreds of clothing left on her. I never saw so many horrified people before."

By August 20, the tally had begun. In Naugatuck alone, 2,000 people were displaced.

Connecticut National Guard units raced to undertake rescues. Units of the 103rd Anti-Aircraft Artillery Brigade from Bridgeport, gunned their trucks for home, leaving an exercise at Camp Wellfleet on Cape Cod to return to their home armories. As 90 vehicles hastened back from the Cape, trucks from the 102nd Infantry Regiment hauled the Naugatuck refugees to homes in the Beacon Valley Range where they would be fed by the Red Cross.

In Hartford, the floods delayed two funerals, but did not stop a somewhat livelier wedding. Louanne Robson Lacey and Richard Arthur Kay's wedding was scheduled for eight in the evening on Friday at West Hartford's Church of the Redeemer. At seven p.m., the wedding remained uncertain—the bride's dress had not yet arrived, and the bridegroom's parents were delayed. Fortunately, Donald Landon Lacy, the bride's father took matters into his own hands. Driving an extremely circuitous route through West

Hartford, Newington, and East Hartford, Lacy made his way around flooded byways to reach the dress shop on Main Street. He repeated the journey to get back to the church. His arrival coincided with that of the bridegroom's parents who had faced a four hour ordeal getting there from the Hotel Statler.

The immediate rescue work conducted on August 19, gave way to supply drops on August 20. Air National Guard helicopters and trucks delivered medicine, milk and food to stricken areas. They were joined by new helicopters from Marine and Army bases in Virginia and the Carolinas. For areas that could be reached by road, commercial trailer trucks were rented out by the state. Supplies were delivered to town officials and Civil Defense volunteers and distributed by the Red Cross.

Truckers and pilots kept detailed logs of the items they were delivering: "Two thousand loaves of bread to Torrington, five hundred loaves of bread to Camp Delaware in Winchester...four sacks of flour to Camp Jewell...into New Hartford, five cases of evaporated milk..."

On Saturday night, Farmington River valley resident Walter Balazy discovered Yolanda Barolomeo, a five year old girl who had spent the previous 24 hours lashed to a tree with her pet beagle, Tiny. With the wind and floodwaters gone, she had untied herself and was playing in the "sandy rubble" with her dog.

When Balazy discovered her, Yolanda offered up a beaming smile. "I wondered what happened to Mr. Leone?" she asked. Albert Leone, a volunteer firefighter from Farmington had been involved in rescue work the day before. While rescuing the

Bartolomeo family from their home, Leone's boat capsized. Fortunately, the group of seven swam to a nearby roof and flagged down a helicopter which lifted the adults to safety. However, before Albert, Yolanda, and her siblings could be airlifted out, the roof broke up. The firefighter lashed the girl and her dog to a tree, before he was swept downstream while the other children sheltered in nearby trees. Fortunately, Leone and the entire family made it to safety once the flood subsided.

In spite of the severe devastation across the state, many Connecticut residents still believed that they were better off than people living in Central Massachusetts. Neither region could claim to be particularly well off, as a result of the storm, but in one key aspect the people in Connecticut were right. Virtually all of the state's water supplies had miraculously avoided contamination during the floods. The same could not be said for Worcester's North End, where 11,000 families lacked clean water after a water main fractured. The Army attempted to counter the problem by issuing vast quantities of water purification tablets and C rations to stricken families.

Worried residents in the greater Hartford area telephoned the Metropolitan District—the city's water supply agency. According to William Wurts, the agency's director, "It [the water] is perfectly safe as far as we can tell." In fact, he added that the reservoirs were in better condition than ever, topped up with a huge influx of freshwater from the skies.

In Manchester, August 20 and 21 blurred into one long slog of a day. Amateur radio operators deployed to replace exhausted emergency radio crews. The first crews that they were replacing had helped to reconnect the community with Hartford and Torrington by the airwaves. An additional radio operator was flown by a Civil Defense helicopter to Torrington, setting up a three way relay between Torrington, Farmington Avenue in Manchester, and the local municipal building. Civil Defense workers stayed at the posts into the third day of the disaster in an example of incredible devotion to emergency work.

As the disaster extended into its second day, a second major fire wracked the small city of Putnam in the northeast corner of the state, recipient of flood waters from upriver – which had already devastated Southbridge, Mass. The city had been "[rendered] absolutely helpless" due to flood waters.

The first fire had engulfed the Uncas Finishing Co. and Putnam Finishing Co. in the Mechanicsville section of town. The two factories had 40,000 and 20,000 gallons of fuel oil, respectively, stored in their basements which quickly ignited.

Rising waters were responsible for the second fire, at the Magnesium Selling Corp. Magnesium is a highly reactive metal that never appears in nature in its pure form. The pure form, stored in barrels in Putnam was slated for use in incendiary bomb making. Magnesium reacts explosively with water, and so the results can be imagined when the Quinebaug river flooded the warehouse.

Flames from the magnesium warehouse and from the fuel oil fire towered into the sky. According to reporters, smoke was visible from 20 miles away. One observer working in Putnam at the time saw barrels of magnesium floating downstream in the flooded Quinebaug River, slamming into submerged rocks and exploding like depth charges upon contact with the water. Firefighters were dropped in by helicopters but were soon forced to retreat by the intensity of the blaze.

By August 20, the situation had deteriorated in Windsor, leading to the evacuation of 130 children from Camp Marlin, along the Farmington River, to the Poquonock Elementary School. A rescue helicopter was dispatched to the Farmington River to search for two policeman who had not reported in for two hours. In fact, the two men were safe— they were simply herding a farmer's cows to safety.

Avon, Connecticut found itself completely isolated from the outside world. Without power or supplies, a call was put out for helicopters. A polio and a pneumonia patient were each airlifted out, along with people trapped on roofs. Health departments in many different communities issued warnings for well-owners to boil their water, while Governor Ribicoff instructed pharmaceutical manufacturers and pharmacies to conserve their supplies.

The worst flooding occurred on Thursday, Friday and into Saturday, August 20. But Sunday, August 21 brought exciting news: flood waters had begun to recede overnight. Falling waters would speed the delivery of supplies, the survey of damage, and the hunt for bodies.

Along the Connecticut River, dikes had helped many communities such as East Hartford to emerge almost unscathed. Local police and firefighters watched the dikes around the clock, armed with rescue boats, walkie-talkies, and generators in case of any leaks. In the Hartford area, three small dams broke during the Friday disaster. Two thousand tons of trap rock were dumped at the Scotland Road Bridge to stop culvert erosion.

In Glastonbury, police watched anxiously as water levels dropped. The stocks of some of the stores in the downtown had been moved to higher ground on Friday, August 19. It was a good decision by local officials. The rising Salmon Brook had swallowed several service stations, shops and a restaurant on Spring Street and Main Street later that day. Outside of the downtown, most of Glastonbury had fared well during the floods. Some of the town's tobacco crop had been ruined, but the seaplanes at the Riverside seaplane base in South Glastonbury (the ones that had not been flown out before the storm) remained lashed safely to trees on the bank.

New Britain and Middletown experienced a more modest impact from the storm, much like Glastonbury. A one million dollar disaster estimate was placed on New Britain where hundreds of basements and some shops were flooded. However, it was comparatively light damage compared with the small city of Thomaston in western Connecticut, which experienced damage greater than four million dollars. Already, over 1,000 people were returning to their homes in New Britain. The city's Stanley Works steel mill was set to reopen Monday after water was drained from its basement. New Britain's A.W. Stanley and Willow Brook swimming pool remained shut, as the only longer term local casualties of the storm.

In Middletown, the Connecticut River crested 23 feet above its normal level, leading to the evacuation of 50 people by the Coast Guard. Some of the town's roads, namely those to Saybrook and New Haven, remained open, but all other byways were shutdown. The town was snarled with traffic during the day as people came to sightsee and buy from the local stores that were still open. Adding to the traffic mess, Middletown was a major stopping point on the route to Boston, and much of the through-traffic from New York City to the rest of New England was passing through the downtown. While local clean-up work went on, city recreation directors solicited donations of 75 cents a head for 400 children to go by train to Ocean Beach Park in New London.

Elsewhere, in Norwich, officials cast nervous glances at the Shetucket River throughout Saturday. Parts of Rte. 12 and Occum's Flats had flooded, but on the whole, the valley had escaped the worst of the floods. The roadway to Jewett City was closed, with police routing travelers over Rte. 163. Along the Thames River in Norwich, shopkeepers busied themselves removing merchandise from basements that could flood as water made its way downstream.

While shopkeepers and police wrung their hands, a group of 31 Hartford children were having the time of their lives. Eleven boys and 20 girls were airlifted by the Air National Guard out of Camp Sholom in New Hartford. The small Jewish day camp had one overnight day a week. That day happened to be Thursday, at the same time that the hurricane arrived. A pond at the camp overflowed and knocked out power. Sholom Bloom, the camp organizer, attempted to drive the children back to the city, but was turned back to Avon when he reached Winsted. In Avon, the Congregational Church opened its doors to the girls, while the boys camped out at Willard Jopson's private residence.

After National Guard helicopters dropped their loads in the Winsted area, they ferried the children five or six at a time to Bradley field, to meet up with their parents. Many of the children reportedly asked when they would have a chance to ride in a helicopter again. The answer: the next hurricane!

On Sunday, enough people had been rescued that Civil Defense was able to turn its efforts to recovery in the Naugatuck River valley, particularly in the communities of Naugatuck and Waterbury. Cheshire volunteer firefighters hauled hundreds of gallons of drinking water into the Waterbury area, which was facing problems similar to Worcester's North End. Cheshire loaned Naugatuck the emergency generator from its town hall, while the volunteer fire fighters simultaneously delivered clothes collected by the Red Cross. Fire engines took turns pumping out basements after deliveries were made.

According to Civil Defense, Cheshire had been "very fortunate;" so fortunate that they were able to help out neighboring communities. Cheshire residents weren't the only ones. One of the many remarkable survival stories from the floods came out of Waterbury, where brothers Archie and Gustave Kramitz accidentally forged into high water with a truckload of vegetables and a trailing passenger car. Gustave's truck stalled in the water, and Archie pulled into a nearby gas station to wait for him to get it restarted. The two brothers were stunned to find water rising around *both* vehicles. They escaped to the roof of the gas station. A man across the street noticed their plight and hauled them to the safety of his second floor room with a clothesline. Both the car and the truck were carried into the Naugatuck River.

When reporters and outside rescue crews reached Waterbury, they were in for a surprise. The city's level of devastation was incredible. Most remarkable of all was the way that the ordinarily tame Naugatuck River had risen so rapidly. One city firefighter commented, "We thought the world was coming to an end." The firefighter's family had been completely separated during the storm, but miraculously reunited as the waters started to recede. "God must have willed it that way." Unfortunately, his neighbors were not so lucky. Most of them were still missing, many presumed dead.

Across the state, the damage tally begun on Saturday continued. By Saturday night, the State Highway Department was able to report 33 bridges destroyed on 12 different state highways. The survey was, in fact, largely inaccurate, with reports coming in from helicopters during daylight only. The tally of bridges destroyed did not count the larger number of blocked roads and flooded (but still intact) bridges.

Thirty construction contractors were put on standby until the Highway Department could give the go ahead to begin rebuilding bridges, a process that could only start after floodwaters receded. Meanwhile, the Army shipped in six Bailey bridges—temporary bridges widely used for conveying troops and trucks over rivers in World War II and Korea.

At the local level, many towns gave the go-ahead before the State Highway Department. By Sunday, bulldozers and trucks were clearing the scrambled remnants of the local highways from the main streets of Thompsonville, laying down gravel in its place. The partially restored road would open up the route to Suffield on the west side of the Connecticut River.

Thompsonville had fared better in some respects than others. According to Dr. Bernard Dignam, the local public health director, public water supplies had escaped contamination. Nonetheless, he recommended a continued boil water order, and immediate typhoid vaccinations for the town. When floodwaters receded, local property owners discovered buckled foundations and crumbling sidewalks.

In Stafford Springs, floodwater had produced similar results. All of the businesses on the south side of Main Street along the Freshwater Brook, were declared temporarily unsafe and off-limits until a state engineer could arrive for an inspection. Most of the town's stores had lost all of their merchandise—not surprising considering that some parts of the town were under 10 feet of water. Early estimates suggested more than five million dollars damage in the town. Connecticut Filter Corp., Stafford Worsted, and three other local manufacturers suffered serious damage.

For some people, the ordeal that was just ending in other communities was just beginning in their own backyard. In Cromwell, 40 families were moved to higher ground and fed at the town hall, when waters rose unexpectedly late on Saturday night. The operators of the Chester-Hadlyme ferry across the Connecticut River to the Gillette Castle called off service due to electrical service interruptions and exceedingly high water in the river.

As many of Connecticut's citizens battled for their lives, representatives from the state met in Peterborough, New Hampshire to agree on watershed councils. The state delegation—the Connecticut River Watershed Council—was led by Ward Duffy, editor of the *Hartford Times*, called for careful conservation efforts. The efforts would involve reforesting the banks of the Connecticut and other major rivers to prevent erosion and limit flood damage downstream. Another Connecticut resident, Professor Paul Sears from Yale told the meeting, "[there is no such thing] as 'flood control'—the best we can hope for is a reduction of the flood hazard." He added, "The flood plain is just what its name implies, and its use by man should be regarded as a risk to be taken with open eyes and not an excuse to charge the damage bill to an already burdened taxpayer." The meeting, scheduled in advance to unveil new thinking about flood control and rivers could not have come at a better time for its lessons to gain traction.

Human names were first assigned to hurricanes in 1950, but the names were universally female until the introduction of male names in 1979. At least one person at the time of the storms, Republican Senator Thomas Kuchel from California, objected to naming storms after women, "[who have] historically symbolized tenderness, devotion, sympathy, and peacefulness." Kuchel addressed a letter to Francis W. Reichelderfer, the chief of the Weather Bureau. "At the same [the previous storm-filled week] I have begun to appreciate the resentment against the Weather Bureau for adopting girls' names to identify successive hurricanes...On occasion they may be stirred by fury, but their rages seldom last as long as 'Hazel's' in 1954 or wreak such vengeance. They can be moody and unpredictable, though rarely as determined as 'Connie' last week. While now and then excitable, few of them show the wrathfulness of 'Barbara' in 1953 or 'Edna' last summer."

In fact, while Barbara and Hazel were not among the "sisters" that struck the Northeast or New England, they were both powerful storms that had a significant impact on regions far north of hurricane breeding grounds. Barbara formed on August 11 in the southern Bahamas, struck eastern North Carolina as a Category 2 storm, and curved back out to sea, passing well to the south of New England but still managing to provide the region with a good soaking and a preview of Carol and Edna. Hurricane Hazel, which followed Carol and Edna in October of 1954, was the deadliest and costliest hurricane of the year, striking the United States near the border between North and South Carolina, as a Category 4 storm. It caused 95 fatalities in the US and another 81 fatalities, when its powerful remains crashed into the area around Toronto, in Canada.

While Kuchel mused about womens' character and hurricane names, Reichelderfer explained to the press that the Weather Bureau assigned hurricanes simple, recognizable names. He suggested that a possible alternative to women's names be by Indian tribe names, such as "Algonquin" or "Winnebago," or perhaps figures from mythology such as "Apollo," or "Zeus." "Of course, you would have to skip such sweet-dispositioned characters such as Apollo and Eros," Kuchel chimed in.

The irony of Hurricane Diane is that it was not, in fact, a hurricane when it reached New England. Lawrence Mahar, the lead meteorologist at Bradley field, told reporters that by the time Diane reached Connecticut, it was a burnt out, extra-tropical storm. But it still packed a very serious punch in terms of rainfall. The *Hartford Courant* announced, "Hurricane Diane never reached us, but she left her calling card in the form of the most violent deluge in recorded history in this area." All told, Hartford, Connecticut alone was drenched with 13.97 inches of water in the space of 30 hours—a new rainfall record. For comparison, the previous record set in 1938 in the Hartford area was 6.7 inches. Diane's extra-tropical character made it a particularly unexpected threat for a region anticipating high winds and storm surges rather than deadly flashfloods. Regional damages in the billions were already estimated by the second day of the floods.

Although Connecticut witnessed the worst of Diane's fury, other parts of the US shared in the misery of the storms arrival. Like the Naugatuck and the Quinebaug, the Delaware River in eastern Pennyslvania overflowed its banks, notably in the small city of Easton, north of Philadelphia and flooding took place throughout eastern Pennsylvania and western New Jersey. The Delaware River Valley and the adjacent Poconos Mountains witnessed the worst flooding since records were kept (a record that appears to hold to this day). Raging waters knocked down 30 dams and destroyed 150 rail and road bridges. In the small community of Stroudsburg, a single dam burst claimed 37 lives as it tore through a summer camp.

In greater Worcester, people were dismayed with the seeming lack of meaningful prior warnings from government and news meteorologists, about the rains and the threat of flooding.

"The river communities of southern New England have long since come to know the meaning and peril of floods. These towns and cities are usually ready for them—aided by the well-developed science of predicting the crest level to be expected and the time that it is likely to arrive. But the floods from hurricane storms like the one which has brought so much havoc to this area in the past 48 hours are something new."

The author of the editorial recognized the difficulty of preparing for a storm like Diane. "These rains are evidently harder for meteorologists to predict than the hurricane winds that sweep up from the Caribbean...even if we had known in advance of the violence and the duration of the Thursday-Friday rainstorm there would have been little that most of us could have done in preparation. Our communities—and in a good many cases, our homes—simply haven't been planned to withstand such inundations."

"From now on, though, we shall certainly take more account of such possibilities. As it becomes more indisputably evident that New England lies in the hurricane belt, precautions must take account of water as well as wind."

Charting Diane

Hurricane Diane Rainfall - August 17-20, 1955

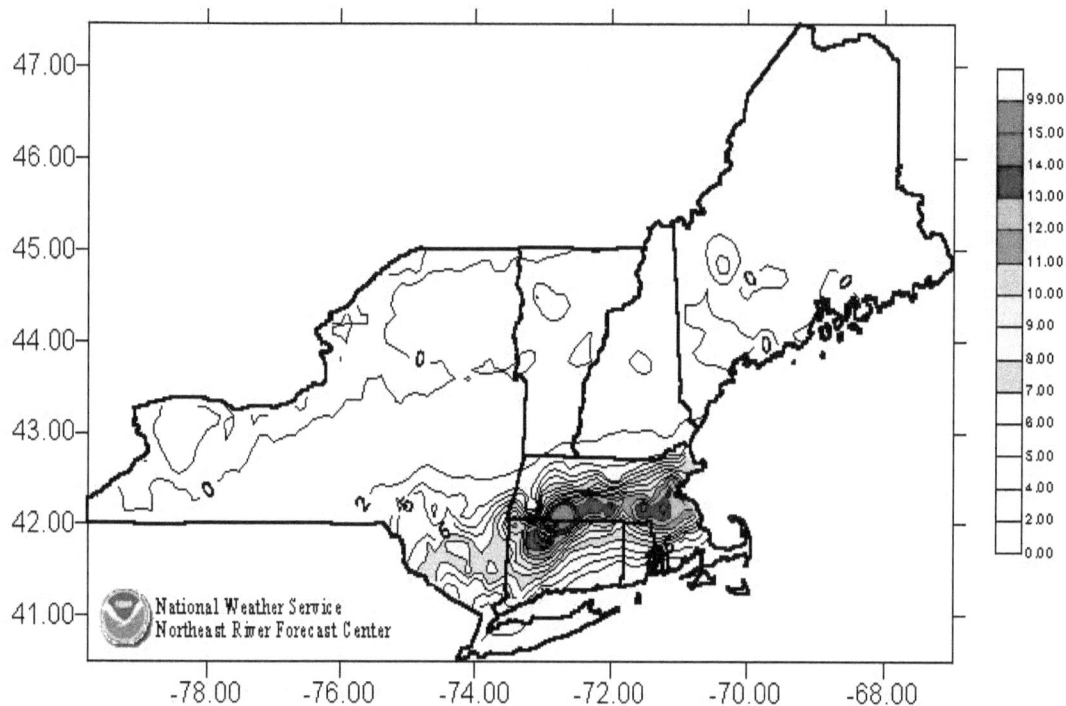

August 1955 Rainfall Accumulation

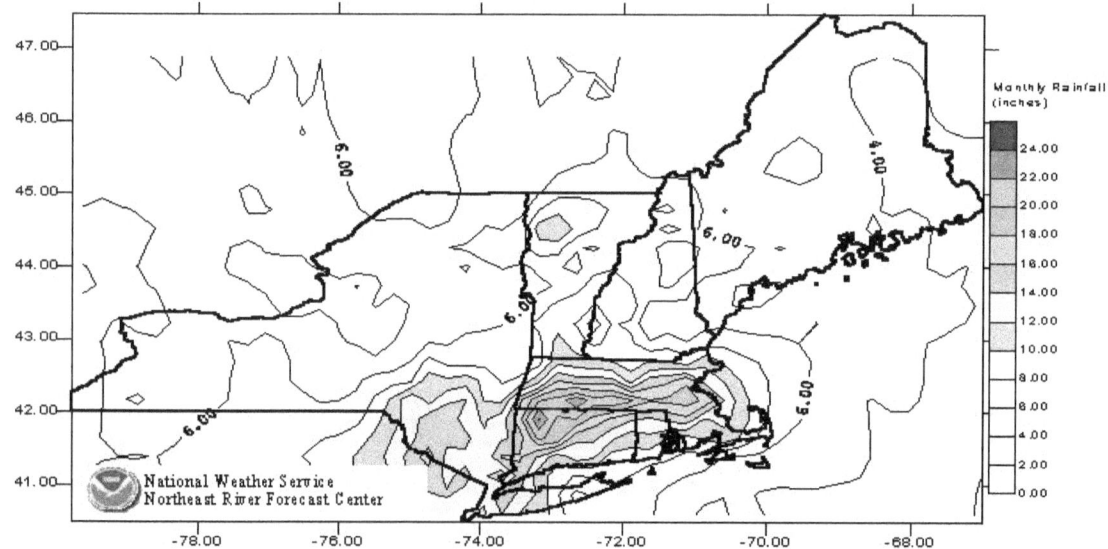

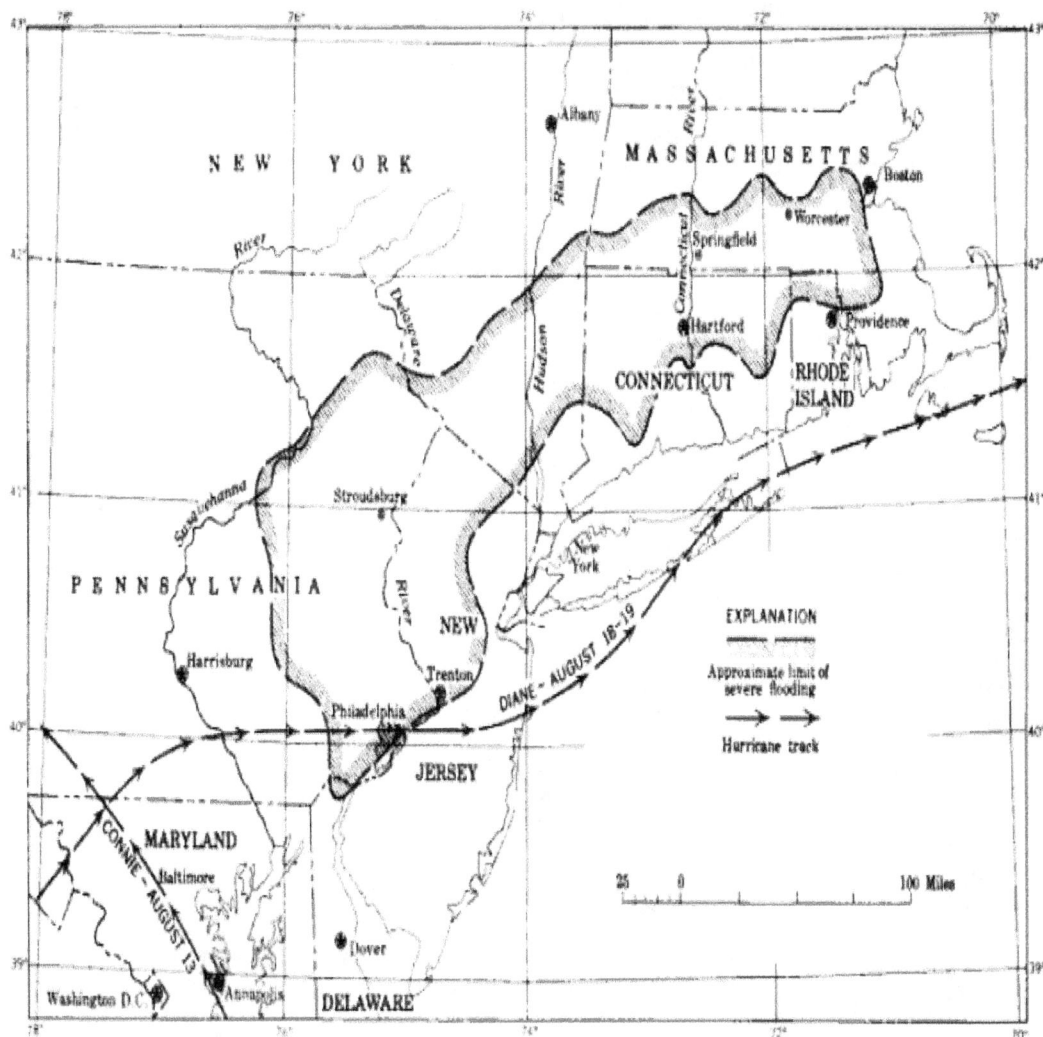

The graylighted highlighted area on the map shows all of the areas that experienced flooding during Diane, along the East Coast (Courtesy USGS)

Devilish Diane: August 1955

Hurricane Diane outdid the destruction of Carol and Edna by large measure, when the storm struck in late-August, 1955. Rhode Island and parts of Massachusetts were spared from some of the heavy damage witnessed during Hurricane Carol, but damage was tremendous across much of Central Massachusetts, parts of New Jersey and Pennsylvania. Connecticut was perhaps the hardest hit of any state, experiencing damage that contemporary observers—many of them military officers—described as "wartime." In fact, many compared the damage to small Connecticut manufacturing cities to the damage caused by Army Air Corps bombing runs against Germany's industrial heartland in the Rhine-Ruhr region. Unless otherwise noted, the following images are courtesy of the National Archives and Records Administration in Waltham, Massachusetts, and show detailed 'stills' of destruction in the immediate aftermath of the storm, taken by Civil Defense workers whose job it was to catalogue the hurricane's impact, and the response to it.

Main Street in Winsted is cluttered with debris, including pipes, slabs of cement, and even steel beams. Note the National Guard soldier talking to a woman by the package store in the left-hand side of the picture. The photographer took the picture looking north, opposite the First National Store.

Winsted's Main Street, seen from the rear of the Sterling Home Safe Co. on Willow Street.

Living up to its name, the Mad River (a tributary of the Housatonic) rages through downtown Winsted at the New England Knitting Mills. This photo was taken behind Main Street.

The gutted ruins of the Metal Selling Corporation's mill stand alongside the Quinebaug River in Putnam, Connecticut. The building was storing drums of highly-reactive, pure magnesium when Diane struck. Magnesium reacts with water, producing high temperature flames. The mill burned as drums of magnesium floated down the river, striking rocks and exploding like depth bombs.

This elderly man appears stunned as he stands by the Consolidated Bleaching Company's burnt out factory in Mechanicsville, Connecticut.

Torrington, Connecticut's town green in the background seems like the only dry place in town.

Looking north on Banks Street, Waterbury, from the US Lime plant. Note the car and the toppled telephone pole in the foreground.

Judging by the pile of wood at the main entrance, the American Brass Company in Waterbury probably sent most of its workforce home.

Pummeled Putnam: August 1955

The following photos were contributed by the Aspinock Historical Society of Putnam and represent the collected photos of many Putnam residents who lived through the storm. The photos provide a detailed record of Hurricane Diane's severe impact on the town.

Water rises around the Putnam Post Office (above) as police and rescue workers wade in below).

A rescue in progress in downtown Putnam, by the radio shop.

Flood stage in the Quinebaug River, as water rushes into downtown Putnam's mills and shops.

Flooded homes in the Monahasset Village section of Putnam. Residents faced some of the worst damage in the town—in some cases even worse than the flooding in the downtown.

A surge of water on Front Street by WINY radio station and Pomfret Street.

A toppled mill leans toward the river off of Bridge Street at the current location of the Putnam courthouse. The area's Eureka mill continued to operate for another five years.

Soggy Southbridge: August 1955

The following images were kindly contributed by Southbridge historian, Richard "Dick" Whitney, founder of Whitney's Southbridge Page and the Optical Heritage Museum. Since the 1990s, Dick Whitney has become a driving force in the movement to commemorate the 1955 floods—and he comes well-armed. During Hurricane Diane, and its immediate aftermath, Whitney's father snapped dozens of photos of local damage and clean-up, including a large number of remarkable color photographs and movie film.

Water rushes into downtown Southbridge (top) and an intrepid driver forges through a rotary on Rte 131 alongside the Quinebaug River (bottom).

This driver took matters into his own hand, forging into the water along the Quinebaug River on the road to Connecticut.

Across the region, Hurricane Diane destroyed hundreds of cars, including this new American car, (above) which seemingly dodged the oil drum in the upper left corner, only to be swallowed up by sediments. The owner of this car was luckier than some. Although his or her engine may have flooded, the freshwater of the Quinebaug River was much less likely to cause serious corrosion than the briny waters of the coastal storm surges in 1954.

The owner of this mangled wreck (above) and the flooded Nash Rambler, (below) are certainly somewhat less lucky than the owner of the convertible on the previous page.

The hardest hit area in Southbridge, the Flats, a traditionally French-Canadian neighborhood, flooded quickly because of its low elevation.

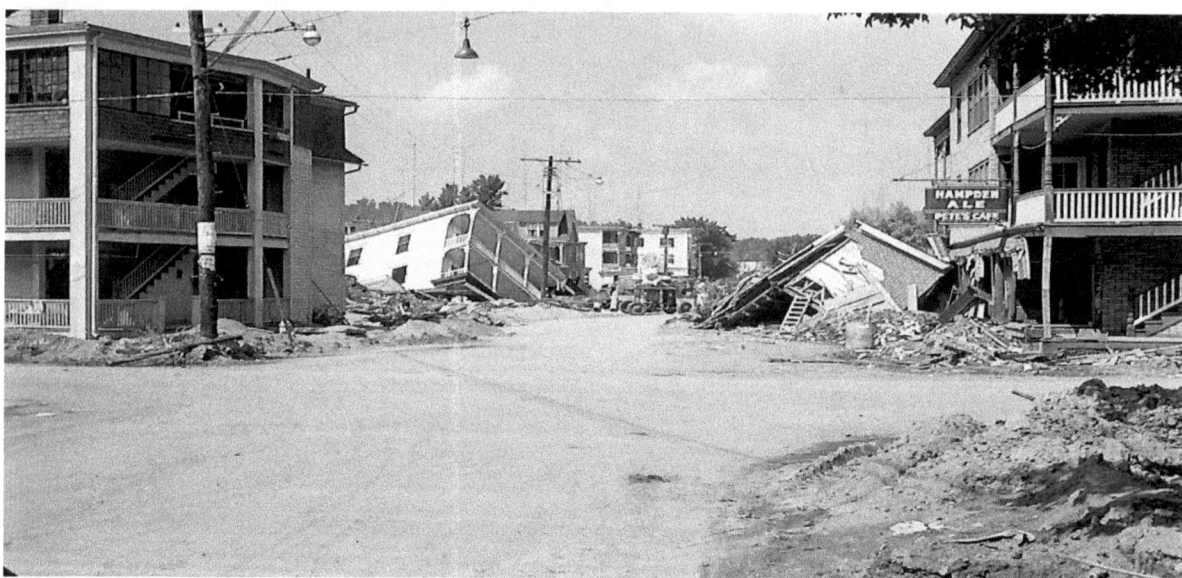

With the water resided, the streets in the Flats are covered in river sediments. Some of the neighborhood's ubiquitous "triple-deckers" were destroyed, including the white building in the center of the picture. However, telephone lines and high-tension lines survived. It's unclear whether Pete's Cafe, at right, survived the storm unscathed. The white apartment building is cleared away by workers (below) as National Guard troops and police look on.

A clam-shell bucket clears away toppled homes while the Southbridge police and the National Guard looks on.

With legions of formula-fed babies throughout New England stuck in locations without power, a small group of valiant milkmen kept deliveries coming, including this driver.

Erstwhile Easton

Diane did more than damage New England. Easton, Pennsylvania was one of several communities in Pennsylvania badly flooded by Hurricane Diane, along the upper Delaware River.

Motorists look west from Highway 22 at the rising waters in Easton.

Looking east on Northampton Street, in Easton's built-up downtown.

Flood waters recede along Northampton Street in the daylight.

Downtown Easton viewed from the railroad bridge over the Delaware River.

The Economic Storm

The 1950s New England hurricanes were among the most economically disastrous storm events in the US at the time. In the years since, hurricanes such as Katrina, Sandy, Andrew and Irene have exceeded the costs incurred by the record breaking 1950s storms. However, the four storms continue to rank among the costliest in US history.

News reports surrounding the hurricanes are replete with tales of economic devastation. Flooded and flame-scarred factories left many workers on long-term furlough and raised questions about whether companies would return at all. Unfortunately, in the years since the storms, very little work has focused on this long-term economic impact.

Unemployment statistics show some possible correlations with the timing of the storms. Throughout the time period of the storms, the federal government's Bureau of Labor Statistics kept up its ongoing effort to collect data on unemployment. Using surveys and questionnaires, the Bureau offered estimates on a monthly basis each year of the 1950s, on a statewide basis.

The results of these studies are still publicly available and merited a second look to see what type of impact the storms had in 1954 and 1955. Newspaper accounts suggest large spikes in short-term unemployment in many cities and towns, particularly along the coast in 1954 and then along rivers in 1955. Certainly many workers were sent home for weeks, and in some cases even months, as their employers struggled to recover.

Statewide trends for Massachusetts across the two years show a slight drop in unemployment between September and November, 1954—the months immediately following Carol and Edna. Many people were put out of work by the storm, but the drop may be due to the clean-up work that followed. Although it is impossible to say for certain, the innumerable broken windows, fallen trees, flooded ground floors and basements may have created abundant opportunities for maintenance and construction workers to clean up in the aftermath of the storms.

It should be noted that the unemployment data only records non-farm laborers: essentially any office worker, shop owner, government employee, factory worker, or maintenance and construction worker. The impact of the storms on farms is less certain. The wind damage to fruit trees, corn and tobacco crops in 1954 may have spurred higher employment for workers in the nebulous, and poorly recorded agricultural industry. The immediate work of removing toppled trees and branches, and hastily harvesting damaged crops may have given way to a period of low-employment during the regular autumn harvest season. However, this is merely conjectural.

The spike in unemployment in Massachusetts in November, 1954 appears to have been unrelated to changes in employment tied to Carol and Edna, although the spike may have been partially the result of the wrap up of repair work and a seasonal spike in unemployment among construction workers as cold weather rolled in. The drop in unemployment of the start of 1955 suggests that mills in places such as New Bedford,

Fairhaven, and Greater Boston were finally "getting on line" once again, ramping up production after decreased production in the aftermath of the late summer disasters.

Unemployment fluctuated throughout 1955, but saw a general increase. However, after August, it rose rapidly exceeding 1954 levels, suggesting commonplace unemployment in some Central Massachusetts mill towns. By the 1950s, growing mechanization of farms in Massachusetts meant that the majority of workers labored in factories or shops, which witnessed severe damage in many locations due to their close proximity to rivers and low-lands. Farms, on the other hand, may have fared comparatively well, absorbing the torrent of rainwater and embracing the lack of wind-damage while their urban neighbors hosed down floors and disentangled flooded equipment.

Federal unemployment data for Rhode Island shows a different pattern than simultaneous changes afoot in Massachusetts. It should be noted that Rhode Island had the smallest workforce of the three southern New England states. Beginning in July, 1954 unemployment rose rapidly and continued to increase until January, 1955 when it experienced a dramatic drop.

Reports in the *Providence Journal* in August, 1954 offer some indication of a possible source for the heightened unemployment. Inclement weather had turned many people away from beaches and seaside towns, forcing restaurants and shops to reduce their hours, tighten their purse strings, and perhaps even furlough workers.

The spike continued into September with the back-to-back storms harming factories, Providence stores and offices, as well as harbors. Although unemployment continued to rise for the rest of the fall, the unemployment rate itself began to drop. The inevitable clean-up and repair work may have been responsible for the change.

Statewide unemployment dropped back to more comfortable levels throughout much of 1955, until Connie and Diane spurred a second, late summer spike that topped 1954 levels. Rhode Island was spared from the kind of coastal trauma that it had witnessed during Carol and Edna, but in the north of the state, around Lincoln, Manville, Burrilville, Pawtucket and Woonsocket, the damage at factories and ensuing month long furloughs for workers almost certainly drove the spike in unemployment.

By contrast with the other southern New England states, Connecticut saw very little change in its unemployment throughout most of 1954. In fact, the only big spike took place between October and December, 1954, and was unrelated to the storms. However, the same could not be said for the autumn of 1955. Between the August storms and the end of the year, unemployment rose without respite, reflecting serious damage at mills and unsteady repair jobs, for many Connecticut workers.

Although the broad economic impact of the storms is hard to gauge, its local impact is comparatively well recorded. For instance, in Charlton, Massachusetts, Hurricane Diane cost the community $1,134,582.34, or almost $10 million dollars in 2014. Seventy families lost their homes or needed emergency aid, at a cost to the American Red Cross of $136,218.57. The flood threatened to exhaust the town's small municipal treasury. To ease the burden, much of the relief money came through Army Corps of Engineers and the State Flood Relief Board.

State money accounted for $769,350.64 of the total, and covered some of the local rebuild including new guardrails and curbs, bridge repairs and stream clearance between Charlton and Southbridge. It also covered the construction of four new bridges, a sewage system for Charlton City, and the rebuild of the Glen Echo Lake Dam.

The Army Corps of Engineers took on the largest burden in Charlton. In Charlton City, the federal government chipped in for $93,750 of $108,750 spent building the new sewage system. Federal money cleared Cady Brook, Little River, and many smaller channels and water mains. It also paid for new highways, bridges, repairs to 14 different roads, the repair of the Ice Pond Dam, and a new dike at the Upper Mill Pond. One rather ominous line item listed $526 for, "Removing [a] house from [the] highway."

In spite of such serious local conditions, many cash strapped communities like Charlton were able to rebuild relatively quickly thanks to a fortuitous combination of generous state and federal aid. The disaster relief money also helped to alleviate local unemployment. In Charlton, as in many other communities, large numbers of contractors and construction workers were hired to rebuild roads, bridges and dams.

Unfortunately, it is difficult to draw conclusions about the storms based exclusively on unemployment data. Unemployment is the result of many different factors and separating the role of the storms is very difficult. Newspaper accounts would seem to suggest that the storms may have spurred lasting economic damage. What is clear is that a comprehensive study of the economic impact of the storms is needed to fully understand their terrifying impact.

One of the best bits of evidence on the economic impact of the storms comes from *Fortune Magazine's* November, 1955 edition. "In a normal August the Naugatuck River of west-central Connecticut is a placid stream, so shallow in places that a boy can wade across it without fear of a scolding at home. But in the uncommon August of 1955...the Naugatuck became the most destructive torrent in New England." The author of the article pointed out that the Naugatuck valley, with its 250 factories and 80,000 workers exported its product all across the nation—and the world. By the '50s, western Connecticut was the nation's center for producing wiring, and for all types of metalworking for copper, zinc, aluminum and brass. Additionally, the region dominated heavy machinery and clock-making, as well as producing rubber boots.

One of the hardest hit producers was American Brass, in Torrington, which employed 1200 people. The plant was submerged under 12 feet of water and sustained $3 million damage. Chase Brass in Waterbury had 2500 employees—even more than American Brass and suffered similar destruction. The region's largest employer, US Rubber, Footwear Division sustained $5 million damage as its factory disappeared under 15 feet of water. US Rubber was forced to idle many of its 5500 employees.

Many factories suffered serious, and often quite bizarre structural damage. Platt Brothers & Co. a small producer of zinc strips and wires was stripped down to its concrete foundation as a result of assaulting waters from upstream and waters rushing through an abandoned power canal. At the Seymour Manufacturing Co. a specialty producer of copper and brass, a number of unused water wheels beneath the floors tore apart the floors when water rushed in. The wheels had to be torn out and buried. Other sites suffered electrical damage, as generators, turbines and motors were immersed. At American Brass alone, 8,000 electric motors had to be disassembled and rebuilt.

Still more factories bore the brunt of river debris, ranging from silt and sand to whole tree and telephone poles, which had to cut up with chainsaws. Some factories even found themselves piecing through wrecked vehicles and corpses inside their factory walls. This "goulash" of debris was particularly evident in the lower levels of American Brass and Chase Brass, where large rolling mill assemblies had to be painstakingly taken apart and cleaned. In factory basements throughout the region, silt filled oil tanks and lubrication lines, which had already overflowed, to cover the sand and flotsam with a thin film of flammable oil.

At least in the Naugatuck valley, manufacturers and employees worked hard to prove that they were stronger than the storm. "The rebuilding began so instinctively that most company leaders never seem to have even considered the possibility of moving." One American Brass executive quipped, "Good grief, imagine our freight costs if we left our big customers and moved South! Besides we wouldn't think of moving. We've been doing business in Connecticut for one hundred and forty years, and that's long enough to have a heritage."

A Gilbert Clock executive had something similar to say. "Our people live right here—we can't move them...We may be damn fools, but we're staying and we're going to be in business where our skilled labor lives and that's right here." Through their efforts, legions of workers expressed similar feelings. Unions set aside wage negotiations as workers poured back into factories to clean aluminum shoe sets, rolling mills and lubrication lines. Even white collar workers rolled up their sleeves to shovel muck out of basements. One US Rubber executive explained, "We weren't going to try to salvage lined gumshoes...but the salvage crews decided they could be saved, so we're going to have about 80,000 pair whether we want them or not."

In a remarkable show of altruism, unhurt factories lent out equipment and repair teams to help their competitors. Waterbury Farrel's President J.M. Schaeffer informed reporters, "It might interest you to know that one company offered to recondition all of our grinding wheels free of charge." Thanks to this remarkable show of force, the Naugatuck valley got back on its feet by Christmas, with most idled workers returning to the production line as early as October 1st. Even more remarkable, the entire process relied on each company's savings, help from other firms, tax savings, and support from the Small Business Administration, rather than flood insurance payouts. American Brass was bailed out by its parent, Anaconda, while smaller companies such as Plume and Atwood, Waterbury Farrel Foundry, and Torrington Manufacturing tapped into their carefully managed savings.

In the aftermath of the floods, manufacturers sought to understand what could be done to prevent similar losses in the future. Many came to the conclusion that the channeling of rivers by industrial activity had contributed to the level of devastation. Channeling and the elimination of wetland areas and building on flood plains had made rivers more "flashy" as they experienced rapid changes in water level. For evidence, planners looked back at damaging floods in 1936, 1938 and 1948, as well as 1955 for evidence. As a mechanism to handle any future damage, some proposed an expanded Civil Defense which would manage the long-term recovery process by meting out federal funds. In spite of the worst natural disaster ever seen in the region, New England's industries bounced back in the aftermath of the floods. But in the grand scheme, the storms had served as another blow to local industries, giving a gentle but forceful nudge in the attrition process that slowly claimed nearly all of the great mills and factories by the 1980s.

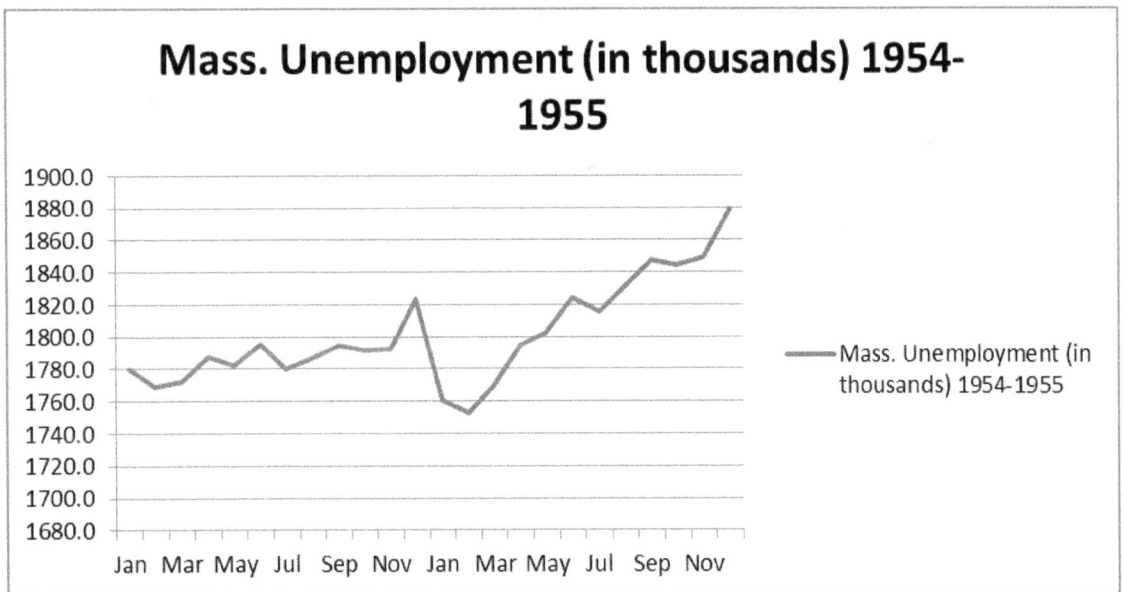

Mass. Unemployment (in thousands) 1954-1955

A line graph titled "Mass. Unemployment (in thousands) 1954-1955" with a y-axis ranging from 1680.0 to 1900.0 in increments of 20.0, and an x-axis showing months from Jan to Nov across two years. The line begins near 1780, dips and rises through fluctuations, drops to about 1755, then climbs steadily to about 1880 by November. Legend: "Mass. Unemployment (in thousands) 1954-1955".

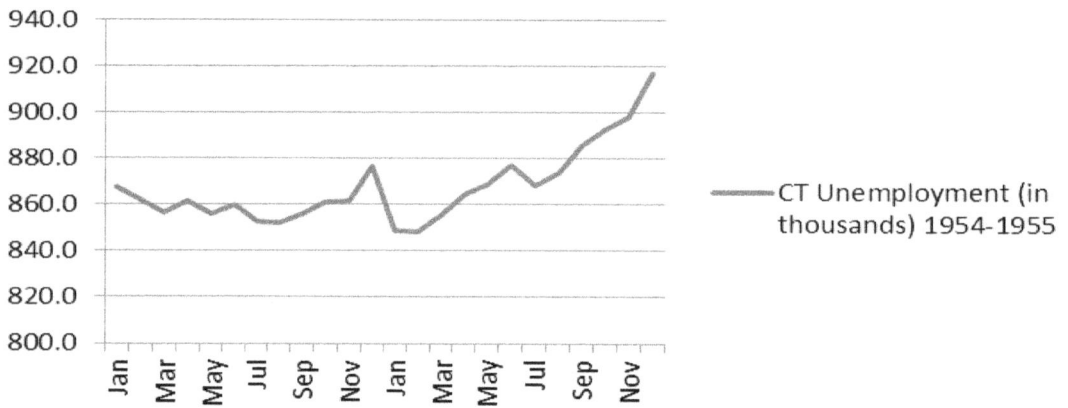

CT Unemployment (in thousands) 1954-1955

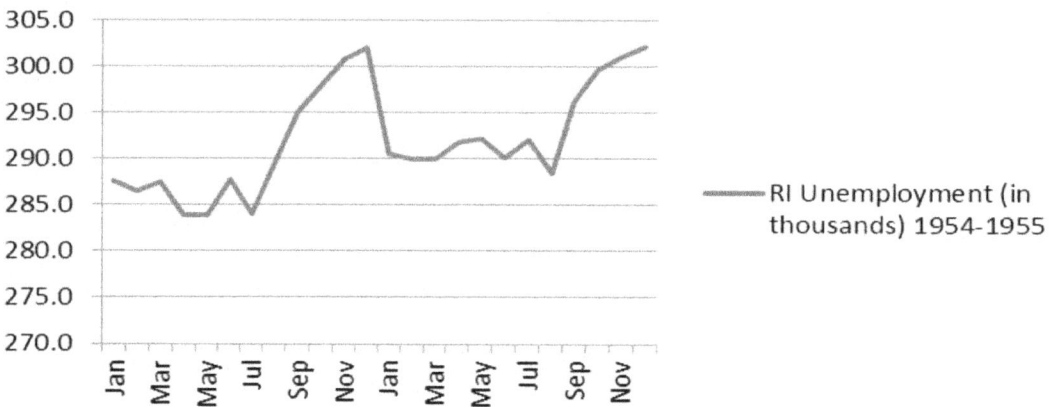

RI Unemployment (in thousands) 1954-1955

Responding to Catastrophes:
The Army Corps of Engineers Remakes New England

The September, 1954 floods and August, 1955 floods New England brought about immediate changes in their wake. "Along with property and life, Diane swept away complacent attitudes toward flood control." As early as 1953, even before the storms, positive efforts had been taken to support regional flood control projects. New Hampshire, Vermont, Massachusetts and Connecticut ratified a compact, that was subsequently approved by Congress, concerning downstream flood control projects on the Connecticut River. Downstream states, such as Massachusetts and Connecticut agreed to recompense the northern New England states for lost economic productivity and taxable property, based on the amount of land that the upstream state had lost to flood control projects.

Unfortunately, the Pioneer Valley agreement proved to be only pioneering. Massachusetts and New Hampshire could not agree to similar measures in the Merrimack River valley. There, a massive twin dam project had been approved in the 1930s, but never constructed. In the New Hampshire legislature the proposed Merrimack compact proved extremely controversial. The House of Representatives in the Granite State cast only 15 votes, out of an assembly of 360 representatives, in favor of a compact with Massachusetts in 1955.

In the immediate aftermath of Diane, the Army Corps of Engineers enacted Operation Noah, a sweeping disaster recovery effort that targeted Connecticut. The Corps was joined by a Flood Recovery Committee set up by Governor Ribicoff, which started the process of damage assessment.

Across the state, they found 668 homes destroyed, 2,460 severely damaged, and 922 farms with serious crop losses. The damage total that the committee tallied ran to $202.8 million. By comparison, the state's total tax revenues for 1955 were a mere $172.2 million. The committee traveled across the state on October 3rd, visiting the hardest hit locations, such as Ansonia, Beacon Falls, Naugatuck, Washington Depot, Thomaston, Torrington, Winsted and Unionville. In a case of astonishing irony, many of the same communities were rocked by destructive autumn floods in the middle of October.

The events of 1955 helped to drive greater consensus on the compact. Massachusetts ratified it in 1956. In Concord, New Hampshire, favorable attitudes began to prevail, due to natural and environmental forces. "The threat of another flood disaster was no doubt a major motivating force." That spring, the Merrimack River basin had twice, or even three times as much water as usual, deposited in thick blankets of snow on the landscape. Spring arrived late, and the threat of a sudden 'warm snap,' and ensuing freshet was almost too much for Fleming, the Army Corps of Engineers' Division engineer, to bear. According to Fleming, if a sudden melt had occurred, or a heavy rainfall arrived, the entire Merrimack River basin, "would have gone down the drain."

Three tense weeks awaited New Hampshire legislators and the Corps. Soldiers and jeeps, many of them from Fort Devens in Ayer, Massachusetts deployed throughout southern New Hampshire conducting reconnaissance to choose the driest and most convenient locations to emplace troops and supplies. Pease Air Force Base, in Portsmouth, New Hampshire became a hive of activity as defense contractors stood by to deliver emergency supplies.

Although tremendous flooding in the Merrimack was narrowly avoided in 1956, the lesson carried over into the following year when the Merrimack River Flood Control Compact was finally passed by a joint session of the New Hampshire House and Senate.

Congress had already taken action in 1956, ordering the Corps to conduct a thorough review of existing and proposed flood control measures for all rivers in the Northeast. The order was accompanied by public funds to get construction started on a number of dam projects that had already been approved, but not acted upon. That year witnessed a new string of projects coming 'down the pipeline' for the Corps. In 1956, work began on three new reservoirs and a local flood prevention project. Each year of the subsequent 10 years from 1956 to 1966, the New England Division of the Corps would start a new project. Work soon began on the Merrimack River twin-dam project and other projects were undertaken throughout the region.

One of the first major projects, launched in 1959 were the Hopkinton-Everett dams, and their accompanying reservoirs in Contoocook, New Hampshire. The Contoocook River is part of the Merrimack River watershed and enters the river five miles upstream of the state capital in Concord. During the early 1940s, the Corps had investigated the Contoocook, and concluded from hydrologic studies that its outflow was one of the biggest contributors to downstream flooding.

Armed with this evidence, Leonard B. Gallagher, then the District Engineer in Boston, had called on workers with the Corps to select the best sites to dam the river and limit its release. Dozens of sites were considered, but none of them were sufficient to 'bottle' the Contoocook's 426 square mile watershed. The problem was resolved by digging a canal through a low lying area between the Contoocook basin and the much smaller (64 square mile) basin of the Piscataquog River.

Two dams were built creating two new reservoirs: Hopkinton Lake and Everett Lake. Nominally, Hopkinton Lake was fed by the Contoocook watershed, while the large Everett Lake drew from the Pisacataquog. In fact, with the addition of a 13,900 feet long canal between the two reservoirs, they could function as a single unified reservoir in the event of high water. Their combined capacity was the largest of any reservoir in New England.

By 1960, the efforts of the New England Division had paid off. The Corps was operating 15 newly commissioned flood control dams, with 11 more in construction. Five other projects were about to begin. The speed at which the projects were completed proved fortuitous. In March, a winter storm piled snow 18 inches—in same cases more— across New England. During the first week of April, temperatures rose and warm rains fell across the region.

Naturally, this sudden warming brought an immediate snow melt, coupled with rainwater. Flood waters raced down the Connecticut and Merrimack rivers. But the flood caused barely a splash. In the Connecticut River valley, seven completed projects and local barriers, together with four others nearing completion prevented an estimated $27.3 million of damage. To the east, similar projects in the Merrimack watershed barred an additional $5.4 million of losses.

For once, Congress and the Army Corps of Engineers had a chance to celebrate some *good* news. Alan K. Sibley, Division Engineer, offered a favorable report to the Chief of Engineers. "The Governors and members of Congress said this was the first time they had received negligible complaints during a major flood and were surprised that it attracted so little public attention." Unlike the calamitous outcome of the 1955 floods, few New Englanders noted the flood waters coursing through the rivers.

Many of the Corps' projects were concentrated in inland, freshwater basins. Although the hurricanes had brought tremendous damage to riverside mill towns and cities, extremely heavy damage had occurred to coastal communities during the 1938, 1944, and 1950s storms due in large part to storm surges. In 1938, for instance, communities along Buzzards Bay experienced tidal flooding 14 feet above average sea level. September, 1944 brought waters 11 feet above to the same area.

The worst outcome of tidal flooding was the immersion of major coastal cities such as Providence, Rhode Island. During the flash flood brought on by Carol in 1954, the city experienced over $40 million in property damage, or about $347 million dollars in 2014. Fortunately, the New England Division stood ready to prevent future coastal devastation.

Between 1961 and 1969, four hurricane barriers were erected in New England. To bar tidal surges from the tapering northern end of Narragansett Bay, Fox Point Barrier was constructed across the Providence River, near the confluence with the Seekonk River.

Fox Point included a 700 foot concrete dam, surrounded by soil dikes stretching 2200 feet. The outer face of each dike was 'rip-rapped' with large stones to prevent erosion and resist waves. The hurricane barrier was built with three gates, each one 40 feet wide. Additionally, a large pump house was added.

During normal weather conditions, the three gates remained open, allowing the river to flow along its normal course, and allowing small craft and barges to pass through. However, the same gates could be sealed shut in an emergency, hopefully blocking the influx of churning bay water. Whatever water accumulated during a storm could be released by the pump house which boasted a discharge capacity of 7,000 cubic feet per minute, using all five pumps. The Fox Point barrier cost $15,844,500 to build in the 1960s,

Just 30 percent of the funds for Fox Point came from local coffers, while the rest arrived in the form of federal dollars. The project began in the spring of 1961 and continued into 1966. Although the Army Corps of Engineers had a long track record of working with civilians, the project reminded military-minded engineers of the perils of working with organized labor. Strikes plagued the project, including a large walk-off at the Tower Iron Works that delayed completion of the third gate. Peter Hyzer, the Division

Engineer in the later years of the project complained that Fox Point was, "[our] number one civil problem."

Curiously, the same was not true for a much larger hurricane barrier under construction to the east. Work on the New Bedford-Fairhaven barrier began a year after Fox Point, but the projects wrapped up at the same time. In fact, the exact *opposite* problem troubled Hyzer in New Bedford. The contractor was so efficient, and led his crews so effectively, that Hyzer was constantly hunting for more money to keep him paid as work forged ahead of schedule. Instead of striking ironworkers, New Bedford harbor authorities threw a 'monkey-wrench' into the mix when Hyzer partially closed the harbor to create an entry channel. Even though a temporary "bypass channel" had been put in place, pilots guiding vessels into and out of the harbor decided that it was too small to get through. New Bedford demanded to know why Hyzer and the Corps were conspiring to strangle harbor traffic! Hyzer raced to the mayor's office, and wrote to the Chief of Engineers later. "This is still a touchy [subject], but I think that local interests are now convinced that the Corps of Engineers is not trying to destroy New Bedford as a port."

The New Bedford-Fairhaven barrier mirrored similar developments in Providence, although it was a much longer structure. Three immense, rip-rapped dikes stretched across the open water at the harbor's mouth. The city's ubiquitous fishing boats and small freighters passed through a 150 foot wide opening in the barrier, that could be sealed shut with a steel gate. The most significant part of New Bedford's seaward defense was the 4,500 foot stretch of dike running across the entrance to the New Bedford and Fairhaven inner harbors. The dikes actually extended farther than the main harbor. Thirty six hundred feet projected to the south, encompassing the outer harbor. Low lying shore areas around Clarks Cove in New Bedford and parts of Fairhaven were surrounded with 5,800 and 3,100 feet of "supplementary" dikes, respectively.

The New Bedford barrier actually cost more than Fox Point to construct, because of its length, coming to $18,614,000 for taxpayers. However, in monetary terms, it may have provided nearly as much value. If the 1938 or 1954 storms ever repeated themselves, Providence would be spared $74 million in damaged and New Bedford $64 million, according to Army Corps of Engineers estimates, at the time.

Two other, much smaller barriers were constructed along the Connecticut shore. The smallest—and cheapest—was a nearly 2,000 foot long earth dike, with additional concrete walls and a pumping station built in Stonington on the Pawcatuck River. At the time, it cost less than a million dollars to build. The other barrier was completed in 1969 in Stamford harbor, and proved its merit in November, 1968, when a nor'easter drove one of the highest tides on record into Stamford harbor. With the enemy at the gate, engineers closed the gate. The gate held, remaining closed for seven hours as the water rose four feet on the seaward face. The barrier was made mostly of earthworks, stretching for 11,700 feet—more than two miles--to protect low-lying areas on both sides of the harbor. However, the barrier still cost more than the maximum damages that it was expected to prevent.

The creation of the Army Corps of Engineers flood control system between the 1950s and the early- to mid-1970s exceeded any previous efforts in the 1930s and '40s to limit flooding. It also drove a trend toward greater integration of information, at the New England Division headquarters in Waltham, Massachusetts. Although some of the projects were placed under local control, the Corps still had a gargantuan task managing two hurricane barriers and 28 inland reservoirs. This kind of management would only be feasible if the Corps could also manage the torrents of meteorological and hydrological data that it received from its stations.

The move to Waltham was completed in 1969 and brought with it great changes in how the Corps' managed its data. Before 1969, data was reported through telephones and radios. It was a cumbersome process that could take several hours to transmit even basic observations from the field. The answer, the Corps believed, was to develop a computerized system.

The Corps worked with Motorola to realize the system first dreamed up by Water Control Branch director, Saul Cooper. The Automatic Hydrologic Reporting Network (AHRN) was operational by 1970.

By early '70s standards, AHRN was state of the art. In New England, 41 battery-packed "remote reporting stations," clung to waterways in five major river basins. Distributed widely, the stations would—hopefully—transmit data by radio signals during even the worst floods and storms. The onboard batteries spared them the risk of power outages. For particularly remote outposts, additional relay stations would guarantee that their transmissions reached the central Reservoir Control Center.

Inland stations along rivers reported on rainfall and water levels in the reservoir and the river itself. Coastal stations submitted somewhat different data, sending along tide levels, barometric pressure, and even wind speed. During normal conditions, each station in the system reported in every six hours. Back at the Reservoir Control Center, a Corps' computer 'gopher' would printout all of the data, a process that took as much as four or five minutes. During severe weather, such as when a station reported a flood or a sudden drop in barometric pressure, indicating a storm, it would report in at three hour intervals. Just in case, controllers were allowed to "manually" call up each station and receive current readings in return. Based on what the stations sent back, the Corps could telephone the operators at the hurricane barriers and reservoir to tell them to open or close the flood gates.

The computerization of the Army Corps of Engineers stations allowed easier data sharing with allied agencies: the US Geologic Survey and the National Weather Service, who were also in the business of monitoring New England rivers. Surprisingly, considering that automation of the Army Corps river gauges took place more than four decades ago, the USGS is still in the process of fully automating its stations in 2014.

Soon, the Corps was looking to improve on the Motorola AHRN system by transmitting to space. The Earth Resource Technology Satellite (ERTS), which was subsequently renamed LANDSAT seemed like an attractive option. NASA launched LANDSAT-1 in the summer of 1972, with LANDSAT-II scheduled to launch in 1974.

The new system would be even more complex than the existing AHRN system. Instead of relaying overland through repeaters, back to the Reservoir Control Center, 27 new data collection centers would be set up to beam the same information about weather and water to space. Once it reached LANDSAT, the data would be relayed to the Goddard Space Flight Center in Greenbelt, Maryland and sent to a clattering teletype in Massachusetts.

However, there was a catch. Teletype machines, dependent on commercial transmission lines, could go down in the event of severe weather, for instance, a hurricane sweeping up the Eastern Seaboard. This would leave Corps effectively blind once again and unable to advise its reservoir crews. In 1975, the problem was solved when a huge satellite dish was erected in Waltham to receive LANDSAT signals directly.

Although the a major test of hurricane preparedness would not come until Hurricane Bob in 1991, New England grew increasingly prepared to deal with flooding rivers in rural locations, with important implications for downstream cities and towns. Meanwhile, expensive preparations for hurricane-driven storm surges helped to guard major coastal cities against serious storm damage.

Barring Future Catastrophes

The following images record Army Corps of Engineers tidal barriers and flood control projects created in the wake of the 1950s New England hurricanes. The images were created by the Federal and are courtesy of the US Army Corps of Engineers.

John Dempsey, mayor of Putnam and advisor to Governor Ribicoff had previously served as a City Councilman and a legislator. In 1955, he helped to coordinate Operation Noah.

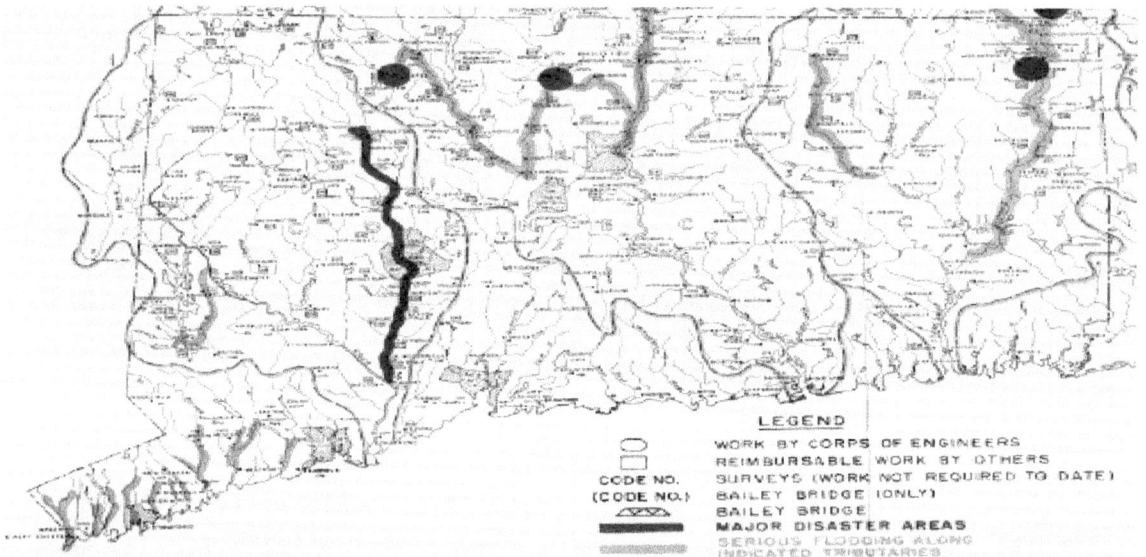

LEGEND

WORK BY CORPS OF ENGINEERS
REIMBURSABLE WORK BY OTHERS
CODE NO. SURVEYS (WORK NOT REQUIRED TO DATE)
(CODE NO.) BAILEY BRIDGE (ONLY)
BAILEY BRIDGE
MAJOR DISASTER AREAS
SERIOUS FLOODING ALONG INDICATED TRIBUTARIES

This Army Corps maps show destruction throughout Connecticut. (Courtesy Connecticut State Library).

Providence's Fox Point Hurricane Barrier was completed in 1966 to prevent a storm surge similar to Hurricane Carol's. It was closed in 1985 for Hurricane Gloria, for 2011's Irene, and 2012's Sandy.

The gates of the New Bedford-Fairhaven flood barrier seen here in the late 1970s.

The gate of the Stamford barrier stays open on this sunny day in the late 1970s. The numerous luxury yachts in the foreground would have to seek shelter behind the barrier during a storm.

An artist's impression of the LANDSAT orbiter used to relay flood control data for the Corps of Engineers.

This view from an intake tower on North Hartland Dam in Vermont shows an upstream view of the Ottaquechee River.

The Buffumville Dam along the Little River in Charlton, Mass. was dedicated August 15, 1958.

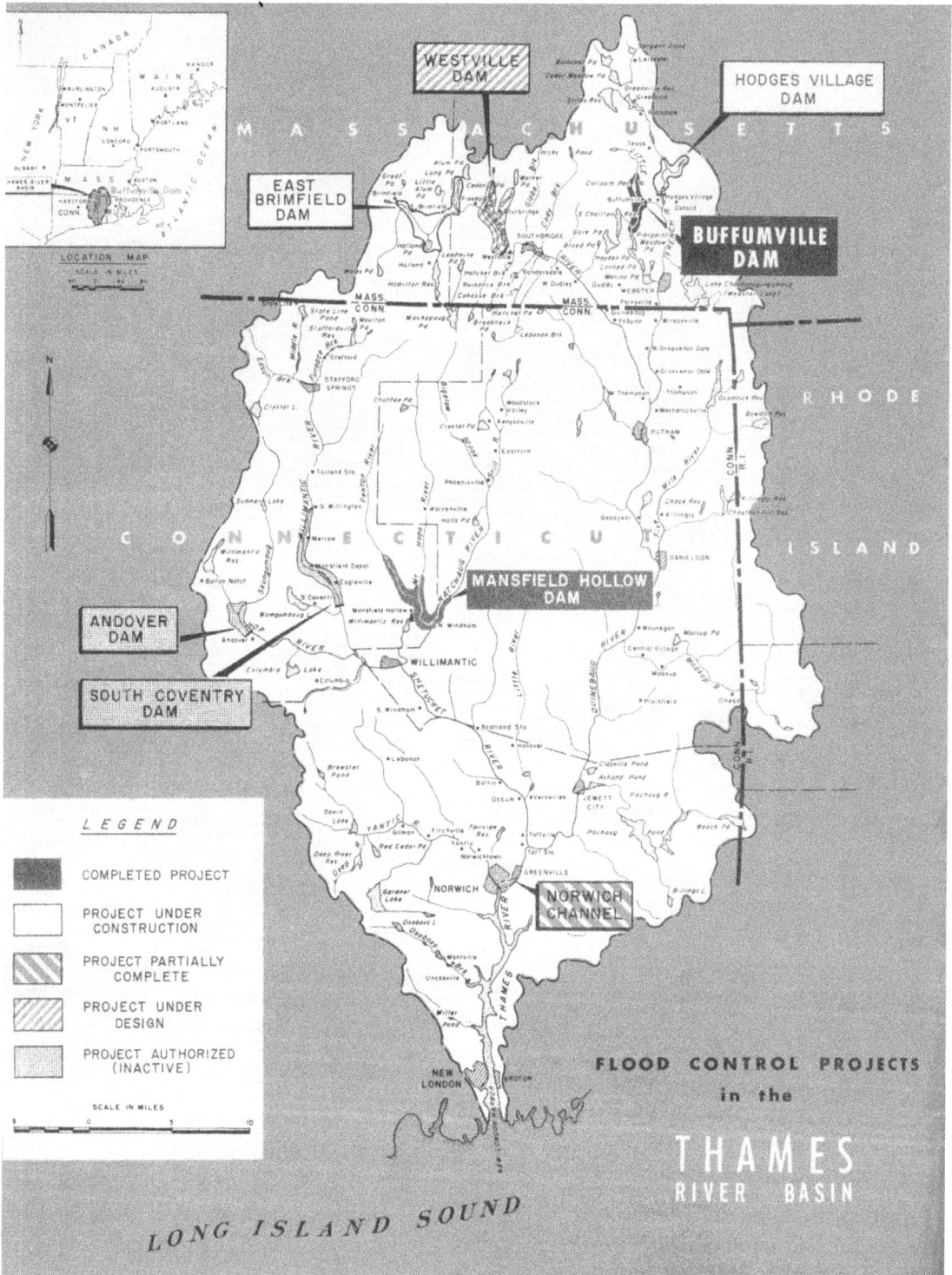

Army Corps' map, circa 1960, shows the Thames River basin, fed by the Quinebaug River, with key dam projects marked.

Damned to the Demon Winds

The Twisted Sisters have passed, but storms like them *will* return to haunt the Northeast. In the Northeast, years and even decades will pass without a serious hurricane. But when hurricanes like the 'Twisted Sisters' do turn up, they do so with a vengeance. Looking in the short term of a single century, the pattern is hard to spot, but it becomes clear once the timeline is extended over millennia.

For reasons that not even the best climatologists can explain, hurricanes strike the Northeast periodically, but there are often long 'dry spells' between the storms. Some mighty hurricanes turn up seemingly out of the blue, like the massive category five storm that slammed Native American villages and Pilgrim settlements in 1635, turning ships in Massachusetts Bay into matchwood.

The earliest 20th century was a quiet period, except for a small hurricane that hit New Bedford and Cape Cod in 1924. Then of course, the spell was broken with another storm on the order of 1635: the hurricane of 1938, followed by the nearly-as-powerful storm 1944. They reminded New Englanders of the incredible intensity and violence and hurricanes -- and the stunning back to back storms of the mid-'50s—the Twisted Sisters— drove home the point (curiously, back to back storms are a recurring phenomenon, recorded also in the late 1600s and in 1869).

1985's Gloria and 1991's Bob served as important reminders that hurricanes did not stop with the Twisted Sisters.

Irene and Sandy harkened back to the Twisted Sisters in 2011 and 2012. Irene knocked out power across New England, and spiked water levels in many inland rivers, though on a smaller scale than Diane. Sandy mimicked Carol with her storm surge along Long Island and the Jersey Shore and Connie's flooding in New York City.

The geography of the Northeast lays out a welcome mat for storms, and some day soon a powerful one—or a family of them—will come knocking.

It's not hard to imagine what will happen. On an ordinary day of the week, perhaps in August or September, the National Weather Service will spot a tropical depression conspiring to create a new tropical storm in the Caribbean. Before long, the cyclonic winds begin to pick up speed, forming an eye, surrounding by swirling clouds. The storms head north, buffeting Puerto Rico, Cuba, and the Bahamas, and grazing Florida and the Carolinas.

As it makes its way north, the storm advisories will begin to go up while the Weather Channel and the National Weather Service chart its course. It will receive a name. Whether it's male or female, it spells destruction.

The storms bears down on the Northeast. From Philadelphia to Boston, people are getting anxious as broadcast channels WCVB, WBZ, WCAU; their cable mates, NECN and NY1, and all of the other news stations share the advice of experts on preparing for the storm. People flock to supermarkets to stock up on food, batteries, and flashlights.

The parking lots of Hannafords, Stop & Shop, Market Basket, A&P, Wegman's, Walmart, Aldi's and Big Y are packed with cars as people make the final dash for supplies.

At FEMA offices and state emergency management offices, tension fills the air, as workers are called in for extra shifts to watch the track of the storm, as it careens out to sea—but not far enough to guarantee that it will miss land. As the final preparations are made, National Guard troops quietly meet at armories in towns across each state in the region.

And then, the storm strikes...

What happens after is the question. Although Gloria and Bob were both strong storms, their strength pales in comparison to the Twisted Sisters. Except in New York, New Jersey, and Long Island, the storms of the 2010s have also been comparatively weak. Inevitably, the Northeast will be hit again, probably by a Category 3 or 4 storm, similar to the Twisted Sisters. But sooner or later, the region will experience the ultimate trial from nature—a Category 5 storm.

The type of storm and the place where it makes landfall will make all of the difference. If the region is lucky, the storm will veer out to sea, grazing Montauk, Martha's Vineyard, Nantucket and Cape Cod, before blowing itself out over the Gulf of Maine. It may be bad news for the residents of these sandy strips, but a few tossed yachts and downed trees may be preferable to the landscape of shattered cities and towns that might emerge if a storm moved even a few miles to west.

So far, the storm barriers built along the southern coast of New England in the aftermath of Carol and the inland flood control areas have stood up to the test of relatively weak storms, but will they stand up to something stronger?

But the Northeast is not quite so lucky today as the storm rolls in in the middle of the night. While people hunker down in their homes for a night of fitful sleep, the wind rises outside. Trees sway, branches break and fly pell-mell through the air. On the shore, high tides combine with the driving waves. In Stamford, Providence, and New Bedford, the Army Corps of Engineers has already closed the barriers. So far, they are holding, although the storm surge laps eagerly at the sea-facing rip-rap.

The wide boulevards of New York, Boston, and Hartford become vast wind tunnels, tearing at small shade trees that line the streets. Debris flies up, smashing car windows. Lights blink out in the suburbs, and backup generators kick in at schools and hospitals. It's time for the National Guard to go into action.

What comes next depends on the strength of the storm, and another key factor—the level of the sea. Global climate change is so frequently mentioned in the news media, that it has joined the background noise of our lives. But many of us don't fully understand what these planet-wide changes could mean for our lives.

The changes may be imperceptible, but they are taking place every day. The morning commute each day into Boston, Hartford, Providence, New York, and Philadelphia contributes in subtle ways to the alterations afoot. Tens of thousands of tons of carbon dioxide pour out of the exhaust pipes of the cars and trucks swarming the highways and the commuter rail trains carrying people into cities for work. Even the power plants that light the office towers and power the computers, printers and fax machines contribute their own unwanted carbon donations.

As the concentration of carbon dioxide, and other greenhouse gases such as methane, nitrous oxide and water rise in the atmosphere, they continue to trap the sun's incoming heat. Ordinarily, this is a very good thing, helping to keep Earth warm enough to support life. But human industriousness has helped to drive these important gases to unhealthy levels. Average temperatures are rising. They may not be rising much, but the change may be enough to kick off large-scale melting of the massive Greenland ice sheet and the even larger West Antarctic ice sheet. Many climatologists and oceanographers believe that this sudden influx of freshwater into the oceans might raise the sea levels around the globe, and induce shifts in weather patterns as oceanic currents stall or reroute.

When most people think of rising sea level, they probably imagine seawater claiming an extra foot of beach sand. But when sea level rises, it rises everywhere, not only on the beach. Particularly in places such as Cape Cod and Long Island, many areas are little than two or three feet above high tide. If a beach house on the outer Cape is only a foot above high tide, then a one foot increase may claim most of the front yard, where sand slopes down to the water. Then, even a small storm surge could be enough to knock the house off its foundation and carry it out to sea.

As emergency planners struggle to get ready, for possible dangers in the future, residents of the Northeast are finding some unlikely allies in the earth science community.

Based out of a two story clapboard lab within sight of Buzzards Bay, the Woods Hole Oceanographic Institution's Coastal Systems Research Group combines the talents of researchers from Brown, MIT, Northeastern, UMASS-Boston, and UMASS-Amherst, to study the storms of New England's past with an eye to the future.

Perhaps surprisingly, none of the people in the Woods Hole group are climatologists or meteorologists. Instead, the team calls on sedimentologists from around the region, who use long aluminum pipes and plastic tubes, and a lot of ingenuity to collect samples of mud from the bottom of coastal ponds, marshes, and lakes.

Jeffrey Donnelly, the lab's leader, and his team, specialize in looking for signs of past hurricanes. In a column of mud that can measure as much as 20 feet in length, the researchers look for a 'smoking gun,' in this case, thin layers of sand mixed in with the soft, goopy brown silt, clay, and algal muck that makes up most of a typical column. The sand is significant—it's used as an indicator of hurricane overwash. Hurricanes drive ashore huge quantities of coastal sand. This was true of Carol, as she buried trucks in Rhode Island to their roofs in sand. Using delicate isotopic dating methods, the scientists at Woods Hole are able to correlate the sandy evidence with historic hurricanes, and storms that happened long before records were kept.

The end goal of the research work is to put together a timeline of storms going back thousands of years that will help the Northeast to get an idea of what to expect, and how to prepare for the changes to come.

The "Twisted Sisters"—Carol, Edna, Connie, and Diane—were unique events, but hardly the once a century storms that they may appear. Even in the wake of 2011's Hurricane Irene and 2012's fiercely destructive Hurricane Sandy, the Northeast is not typically regarded as a center for hurricane activity. With the exception of 1991's Hurricane Bob and the storms of the 2010s, few major, recent tropical cyclones have impacted the region. Instead, most of the serious hurricanes have slammed into Florida, the Carolinas, or the Gulf Coast; storms such as Hurricane Andrew (an incredibly rare Category 5 hurricane that hit Florida in 1992) and Hurricane Katrina in 2005.

The 1950s storms reaffirmed the lessons of 1938 and 1944—that New England shares the South's vulnerability to hurricanes--and the recent storms have served as a reminder. The storms that struck New England were strong, but not uncharacteristic (such as the rare, Category 5 intensity of Hurricane Andrew). In fact, in an ironic twist, the least destructive of the four storm was Connie, which achieved the greatest intensity, weighing in at Category 4. In the wake of the storms, New England, rather than the South, became one of the nation's leading recipients of federal disaster aid and flood prevention spending throughout the 1950s and 1960s.

New England leveraged its large representation in Congress at the time to push for greater accountability for the Weather Bureau, and better technology, such as Doppler radar to predict future storms. Although widespread damage was certain to occur with the arrival of Hurricane Carol, the Bureau's failure to accurately predict the storm and warn the public made the losses more severe. The same New England bloc pushed for Army

Corps of Engineers involvement that would go beyond simply fixing the damage. Instead, the Corps would have to prepare to *prevent* damage in future storms.

Throughout the 1950s and '60s, the geography of interior and coastal New England was reworked in some locations with the construction of flood control dams, flood plain storage areas, and tidal barriers.

To date, the Corps' civil engineering prowess has proven largely effective against the storms that have traveled toward New England. Although heavy rainfall and high winds could still produce some damage, the regional cities of Stamford, Providence, and New Bedford are now protected against storm surge, barring any unforeseen failure of the tidal barrier. However, smaller coastal communities and low-lying areas remain unprotected against storm surges.

The modern Northeastern US is to some extent, *less* prepared to cope with hurricanes than during the 1950s. Even though infrastructure has been constructed to deal with flooding, the record of the storms shows much of the damage—and even many of the deaths—resulting from local flooding of lowlands and trees falling on homes, cars and power lines. The proliferation of forests and the loss of farmland has accelerated since the 1950s, pointing toward lower overall agricultural damage. But in the same time frame, reliance on electricity has continued to grow. By the 1950s, electrification and appliances were already entrenched traditions, but many homes still had kerosene lamps, candles, and ice boxes ready to substitute for the glow of light bulbs and the reliability of a refrigerator. The story of milk suppliers in Rhode Island reverting to the old methods of the 1920s and

'30s, milking their herds by hand during Carol and Edna is a testament to the adaptability of the people who lived during the 1950s storms.

Decreased reliance on land-line phones means that during a contemporary storm, people are able to continue to communicate for a few days, even during periods of blackout while storm recovery takes place. However, other infrastructure has become increasingly reliant on electricity, for instance the ubiquitous supermarkets that now dot the landscape. Perhaps most concerning, is the disappearance of the Civil Defense system. Although the recovery from the storms of the 1950s was slow, it was sped up in the Northeast by large numbers of National Guard troops and civilian Civil Defense volunteers, who set up shelters, patrolled the streets, distributed supplies and cleared debris. However, the primary aim of Civil Defense was actually to undertake disaster relief in the event of Soviet nuclear or chemical attacks. Since the end of the Cold War, this organized body of trained responders has disappeared completely, leaving only a small cadre of non-deployed National Guard units and hastily organized volunteers to respond to a storm.

References & Notes

Introduction

- Schlesinger, M.E. (1994). "An oscillation in the global climate system of period 65-70 years." *Nature* 367 (6465):723-726.

Hurricane Carol

- Staff. "Stalin Auto Plant Uses R.I. Tools," *Providence Journal*, August 28, 1954.
- Sherwood, Kay, "Work Outside in September," *Providence Journal*, August 25, 1954.
- Staff. "Westerly's Beach Merchants Term Summer a Dud," *Providence Journal*, August 1, 1954.
- Advertising. "Hurricane warning! Dealers take shelter." *Providence Journal*, August 6, 1954.
- Staff. "Shipping Warned, Craft Flown Out of Quonset, Tuna Derby in Doubt as High Winds Head for R.I. Coast," *Providence Journal*, August 31, 1954.
- Staff. "Hurricane Carol Hits North Carolina Shore," *Providence Journal/Associated Press*, August 31, 1954.
- Staff. "Warning Late on Hurricane—Hub Bureau Advisory Given Only Half Hour Before Arrival," *Providence Journal*, September 1, 1954.
- Warner, Norman J., "Westerly is Badly Battered; Nine Are Reportedly Missing," *Providence Journal*, September 1, 1954.
- Staff. "Electric Power Out in State: Prospect of Restored Service Today Dim; Work Crews Imported," *Providence Journal*, September 1, 1954.
- Staff. "3 Men Save Janitor Locked in Garage by Rising Flood Tide," *Providence Journal*, September 1, 1954.
- Staff. "Private Forecast Gave UTC 5-Hour Warning of City Flood," *Providence Journal*, September 1, 1954.
- Hale, Stuart O., "Devastating Blow, High Tides Mash Houses, Piers, Boats," *Providence Journal*, September 1, 1954.
- Staff. "Business Boom Follows Storm," *Providence Journal*, September 1, 1954.
- Staff. "Insurance Firms Act on Flood of Claims," *Providence Journal*, September 1, 1954.
- Staff. "Floods Cripple Postal Service," *Providence Journal*, September 1, 1954.
- Staff. "Milk Supply Near Normal," *Providence Journal*, September 1, 1954.

- Martasian, Paul, "Business and Industry Returning to Normalcy," *Providence Journal*, September 7, 1954.
- Staff. *Hartford Courant*, August 28, 1954.
- Christensen, Robert, "8 Girls Ride Out Storm on Two Masted Schooner," *Hartford Courant*, September 2, 1954.
- E. Roy Ray & Ernest N. Dickinson, "Coast Dwellers Flee as Flood Hits Shore," *Hartford Courant*, September 1, 1954.
- Atwood, Frank, "Apple, Tobacco Growers Take Tremendous Loss," *Hartford Courant*, September 1, 1954.
- Staff. "Storage Building Burns at Height of Hurricane," *Hartford Courant*, September 1, 1954.
- Staff. "Hurricane Highlights," *Boston Post*, September 1, 1954.
- Nielson, Hal, "Photographer Describes Survey by Air," *New Bedford Standard-Times*, September 3, 1954.
- Staff. "Gale, High Tide Damage Industrial Plants in City, Wreck Water Craft," *New Bedford Standard-Times*, September 1, 1954.
- Lacaillade, Paul, "NH Repair Crews Busy as Damage Estimates Soar," *Manchester Union-Leader*, September 2, 1954.
- Drury, Robert J., "Big NH Apple Crop is Severely Damaged," *Manchester Union-Leader*, September 2, 1954.
- Staff. "Storm Worst to Hit State Since 1938: Damage to Homes, Crops, Seaside Property Heavy," *Portland Press Herald*, September 1, 1954.
- Staff. "Oxford County Hard Hit by Hurricane with Factories Forced to Close Early," *Portland Press Herald*, September 1, 1954.
- Staff. "Three Quarters of Bath Area Without Power," *Portland Press Herald*, September 1, 1954.
- Staff. "Picnic Atmosphere Prevails as Brunswick Residents Tour Hurricane Area," *Portland Press Herald*, September 1, 1954.
- Staff. "Governor Wires Ike for Cash Grant to Maine Orchardists," *Portland Press Herald,* September 2, 1954.

Hurricane Edna

- Staff. "Northeast Braced for Smashing Blow," *Hartford Courant*, September 11, 1954.
- Staff. "Winds Cut Power, Communications," *Providence Journal*, September 12, 1954.
- Staff. Newport to Take Hurricane Debris, *Providence Journal*, September 16, 1954.

- Staff. Northeast Braced for Smashing Blow, *Hartford Courant*, September 11, 1954.
- Staff. Phone Workers Mobilized for Hurricane Duty, *Hartford Courant*, September 11, 1954.
- Staff. "Milkman Tries to Beat Storm," *Hartford Courant*, September 11, 1954.
- Staff. "Hurricane Twins," *Hartford Courant*, September 12, 1954.
- Staff. "Utilities Begin Trestle Repairs: Railroad, Telegraph, NELCO Crews Work at Barrington Span," *Providence Journal*, September 16, 1954.
- Staff. "Drains 2 Ponds to Remove Salt Water Content in City Water Supply," *Providence Journal*, September 17, 1954.
- Staff. "Water is Safe Official Says: Woonsocket Residents Told Not to Worry about Color and Taste," *Providence Journal*, September 17, 1954.
- Staff. "70-Foot Chimney Crashes Salem Baby Hospital Roof," *Boston Post*, September 11, 1954.
- Rosen, Rebecca J. "The Complaints You've Made About Sandy-Hyping on Twitter and TV, E.B. White Made About Radio in 1954," *The Atlantic*, October 29, 2012.
- Staff. "Electric Firms Make Big for Atomic Power in N.E.," *Providence Journal*, September 17, 1954.

Hurricane Connie

- Staff. "Virgin Isles Feel Hurricane Edge: Puerto Rico Touched; Waters Off Florida Declared Safe Today," *Providence Journal*, August 7, 1955.
- Staff. "Connie 450 Mi. Off Fla. Heading North," *Providence Journal*, August 9, 1955.
- Staff. "Fuller Understanding of Vaccine Plan Urged," *Providence Journal*, August 9, 1955.
- Staff. "R.I. Alerted but Hurricane's Course Continues Uncertain," *Providence Journal*, August 10, 1955.
- Staff. "CAP in Valley is Standing by for Hurricane," *Providence Journal*, August 10, 1955.
- Staff. "2 Towns Ready to Act if Hurricane Strikes," *Providence Journal*, August 11, 1955.
- Staff. "Bristol Rushes Preparations to Fight Connie," *Providence Journal*, August 11, 1955.
- Staff. "R.I Alerted but Hurricane's Course Continues Uncertain," *Providence Journal*, August 10, 1955.
- Staff. "Course of Hurricane Diane Still is Considered Doubtful," *Providence Journal*, August 12, 1955.

- Staff. "Hurricane Diane Born in Atlantic," *Providence Journal*, August 12, 1955.
- Staff. "Rhode Island Gets Hurricane Warning: High Tides Forecast in Area for this Afternoon," *Providence Journal*, August 13, 1955.
- Staff. "Pawtucket Will Mark 'End' of World Strife," *Providence Journal*, August 14, 1955.
- Staff. "State Gets Heavy Surf and Rain as Connie Veers Off to the West," *Providence Journal*, August 14, 1955.
- Staff. "Connie Dies Out Over Lake Erie," *Providence Journal*, August 15, 1955.
- Staff. "Weather Bureau Back to Normal," *Providence Journal*, August 15, 1955.
- Staff. "What to Do Till the Hurricane Dam Comes," *Providence Journal*, August 16, 1955.

Hurricane Diane

- Staff. "Diane's Winds Rake Connie-Beaten Shore," *Providence Journal*, August 17, 1955.
- Staff. "3 Killed in VT. As Rain Weakened Land Gives Way," *Providence Journal*, August 18, 1955.
- Staff. "Child Loses Life Falling in Pond at Charlestown, *Providence Journal*, August 18, 1955.
- Dunbar, Arthur, R., Jr., "Weather Bureau Cites Hurricane Progress," *Providence Journal*, August 19, 1955.
- Staff. "Washout Derails Train; 30 Hurt," *Providence Journal*, August 19, 1955.
- Staff. "Railway Service Disrupted and Roads Flooded," *Providence Journal*, August 19, 1955.
- Marshall, James J., "Water, Rising Foot a Minute, Smashes Social Area Stores," *Providence Journal*, August 20, 1955.
- Staff. "19 Are Saved in Woonsocket by Lifeguards," *Providence Journal*, August 20, 1955.
- Stiles, Edmund K., "Water Rising at Rapid Rate: 2 Spans Closed," *Providence Journal*, August 20, 1955.
- Staff. "Pawtucket Spared Heavy Loss; Slater Mill, City Hall Flooded," *Providence Journal*, August 21, 1955.
- Skow, John A., "Tomorrow Pushes Back Despair," *Providence Journal*, August 21, 1955.
- Staff. "Flood Disinters 200 Caskets From Cemetery," *Providence Journal*, August 21, 1955.
- Staff. "Bride, Washed Out of Home Goes Through with Vows," *Providence Journal*, August 21, 1955.

- Staff. "Blackstone Devastated by River on Rampage," *Providence Journal*, August 21, 1955.
- Staff. "Doomed Buildings in Woonsocket May Leave 166 Families Homeless," *Providence Journal*, August 24, 1955.

- Staff. "Floods to Idle 6,000 in Blackstone Valley," *Providence Journal*, August 21, 1955.
- Charlton Town Report, 1955
- Staff. "Roads Washed Out, Homes Threatened," *Worcester Telegram*, August 19, 1955.
- Staff. "Rainfall Here Topped Only by Last Year's Hurricanes," *Worcester Telegram*, August 19, 1955.—NOTE: Rainfall records kept for Worcester since 1903
- Staff. "Hundreds of Families Evacuated as West St. Dam, Bridges Break," *Southbridge Evening News*, August 19, 1955.
- Parker, Aubrey, *Army Engineers in New England,* p. 195.
- McCarthy Earls, Eamon, *Franklin: From Puritan Precinct to 21st Century Edge City*, p. 142-143.
- Staff. "City Radio, TV Stations Air Many Messages," *Worcester Telegram*, August 20, 1955.
- Staff. "Boy, 13, Held in Break," *Worcester Telegram*, August 20, 1955.
- Staff. "Storm Maroons 200 at Auburn High School," *Worcester Telegram*, August 20, 1955.
  Staff. "Flood Time, 1955," *Worcester Telegram,* August 20, 1955.
- Staff. "38 Believed Lost in Worst Disaster." *Hartford Courant*, August 19, 1955.
- Neuman, Harry. " 'Copter Flier Describes Terror of Flood Victims." *Hartford Courant*, August 19, 1955.
- Staff. "Storm Fails to Delay Wedding After Bride's Father Bucks Traffic." *Hartford Courant*, August 20, 1955.
- Staff. "Child Survives Wild Night Lashed to Tree in Water." *Hartford Courant*, August 21, 1955.
- Staff. "Hunger, Disease Menace Western Massachusetts." *Hartford Courant,* August 21, 1955.
- Staff. "Reservoirs Water Safe, MD Reports." *Hartford Courant*, August 21, 1955.
- Staff. "CD Workers Scheduled to Remain Mobilized." *Hartford Courant,* August 21, 1955.
- Staff. "Fires Raze Large Mills in Putnam." *Hartford Courant*, August 20, 1955.

- Staff. "Families Leave Homes in Windsor Flooding." *Hartford Courant*, August 20, 1955.
- Staff. "Million Dollar Estimate Placed on City Losses." *Hartford Courant,* August 21, 1955.
- Staff. "City Alerted to Possibility of Rise in Shetucket River." *Hartford Courant*, August 21, 1955.
- Staff. "31 Stranded Campers Thrilled by Airlift Ride." *Hartford Courant*, August 21, 1955.
- Staff. "Officials Started Aid for Flooded Naugatuck Valley." *Hartford Courant*, August 21, 1955.
- Zemaitis, Anne. "Waterbury Fireman Tells of Harrowing Experience." *Hartford Courant*, August 22, 1955.
- Staff. "Highway Survey Shows 33 Bridges Destroyed." *Hartford Courant*, August 21, 1955.
- Staff. "Work of Reconstruction of Main Highways Begins." *Hartford Courant*, August 21, 1955.
- Staff. "River Watershed Councils Proposed for New England." *Hartford Courant*, August 19, 1955.
- Staff. "Senator Protests Naming Hurricanes After Women." *Hartford Courant*, August 18, 1955.
- Staff. "Record Deluge Let Loose by Diane's Dying Fury." *Hartford Courant,* August 21, 1955.
- Staff. "National Guard." Hartford Courant, August 19, 1955.
- Staff. "Child Survives Wild Night Lashed to Tree in Water." *Hartford Courant*, August 21, 1955.

The Economic Storm

- Bureau of Labor Statistics: CPI Inflation Calculator.
- Bureau of Labor Statistics. Monthly Unemployment 1954-1955, Massachusetts.
- Bureau of Labor Statistics. Monthly Unemployment 1954-1955, Rhode Island.
- Bureau of Labor Statistics. Monthly Unemployment 1954-1955, Connecticut.
- Saunders, Dero A. "Ordeal of an Industrial Valley." *Fortune Magazine*, November, 1955.

Barring Future Catastrophes

- Blake, Eric S. The Deadliest, Costliest, and Most Intense United States Tropical Cyclones from 1851 to 2010 (and Other Frequently Requested Hurricane Facts). NOAA Technical Memorandum, 2011. Print.
- Parker, Aubrey, Army Engineers in New England, p. 192
- (BLS: CPI Inflation Calculator)
- Parker, Aubrey, Army Engineers in New England, p. 195, 200, 203
- Aubrey, Parker, Army Engineers in New England, p. 206
- Staff. "Report of the Connecticut Flood Recovery Committee to Governor Abraham Ribicoff." *State of Connecticut*, November 3, 1955.

About the Author

(Courtesy Ethan McCarthy Earls)

Eamon McCarthy Earls calls upon his background in historical research and geology to reassemble the story of the great 1950s New England hurricanes. The storms that struck 60 years ago strike a personal note with Eamon, whose family witnessed the devastating 1955 flood first hand in Southbridge, Massachusetts. In addition to his research on the 'Twisted Sisters,' Eamon has worked on New England hurricane research with the Coastal Systems Research Group at the Woods Hole Oceanographic Institution.